PERFORMANCE
Roadsters

First published 1995
© Firebird Publications Ltd. 1995

ISBN 0 9525736 0 1

Published by **Firebird Publications Ltd.,**
1 Howard Road, Reigate, Surrey RH2 7JE
Tel: 01737 222030

Typeset by Crocodile, Crawley
Page design by Jane Burdge
Repro by Digiscan, London
Printed by Quadratek Printing, Newbury

Introduction

If you've ever driven a nicely built Caterham Super Seven, Tiger Super Six or Dax Rush powered by a high output engine, you'll know there's no other driving sensation to match the pure exhilaration felt. If you've sampled the ferocity of a thunderous Westfield SEiGHT or the incredible agility of the Vauxhall 2-litre 16V powered Caterham HPC, you'll know the ultimate in wickedly high performance. Small these cars might be in terms of physical size but, boy, there are virtually no limits to their depth of character and reservoirs of fun.

So it's no surprise that sales of cars like the Caterham, Westfield, Robin Hood, Tiger etc. have blossomed over the last few years. Vast numbers of kit form packages have been enjoyably assembled in leisure-time hours by enthusiasts keen to grab a slice of the action. It is for them and those still thinking about a project, and anticipating the driving sensation, that this book has been written. We hope you enjoy reading it at least a fraction as much as you enjoy the buzz of piloting a performance roadster.

Acknowledgements

All thanks here go to the managements of the companies described in this book and to *Which Kit?* magazine. Everybody at Caterham Cars, DJ Sportscars, Westfield Sportscars, Tiger Cars, Robin Hood Engineering, Sylva Autokits and Vindicators Cars was extremely helpful with historical facts and current information. *Which Kit?* lent its expertise, not only via the sections of the book written by editor, Ian Stent, and publisher, Peter Filby, but also with its layout/production team and vast library of photographs. Cheers, everybody.

Contents

About the Authors...

Monty Watkins is one of the great individuals amongst motoring journalists, a man blessed with cutting wit and a sharp ability for technical assessment. Initiated in auto writing on *Which Kit?* magazine, he took a year-long break to work on a remote Australian sheep farm before returning to become editor of Britain's leading kitcar magazine. Today he is editor of *Fast Ford* magazine whilst still retaining strong links with the kit car scene. He lives in Gloucester.

Editor of *Which Kit?* magazine, Ian Stent did his initial career training in estate management at the Royal Agricultural College at Cirencester. He worked as a land surveyor before joining *Which Kit?* and progressing to management of the magazine. Builder of a superb Sylva Striker, he is an avid enthusiast of lightweight, high performance sports cars.

Peter Filby is *Which Kit?*'s founder and publisher. Famous for his kit car journalism, he was instrumental in his magazine's workshop staff successfully building a Robin Hood S7 and a Caterham Classic, both of which he drove enthusiastically for as long as he could prevent anyone else grabbing the keys. A resident of Reigate, Surrey, he has written and published many specialist car books.

Chapter 1
Background to the breed

Considering the unpredictable, often bad tempered weather we have to tolerate in Britain, it's quite remarkable that open-topped motor cars are popular at all, let alone high-performance chargers that allow wickedly cold wind to blast-freeze your face and radically restyle your hair. That's without considering the welfare of ears, sensitive teeth, watery eyes and unfortunate flies. But popular such cars are – popular with a vengeance.

In driving terms, the breed of performance roadsters described in this book is easy to understand and justify. Pure wind-in-the-hair exhilaration sums-up neatly the type of reward gained from a good blast along a challenging road in one of these machines. Call it simple driving fun if you wish but the experience remains no less rewarding. It's all about acceleration, a responsive chassis, firm ride, top class handling and ultimate road-holding. A carefully engineered feeling that driver and machine are as one.

All very understandable, but why are performance roadsters so small, so basic? The answer is again fairly obvious when considered in the context of all-out acceleration and the sort of response that the enthusiastic driver would normally only get from a purpose-designed racing car. But, historically speaking, there's another reason why the breed is of such minimalistic design and layout.

Utterly fed-up with recession, hostilities and austerity, the post-World War 2 car enthusiast felt a powerful need to eliminate his cares and frustrations with some 'real' motoring. The roads were generally clear, racing events were back on the agenda and the mood was right for fun. The trouble

was that suitable sports cars were either non-existent or priced beyond reach of all but the wealthy.

Then there arrived the concept of the 'special' – hardly a new idea but now one that took on rather a

The Lotus Mk.6 was the company's first serious attempt at volume production and the car soon gathered an enthusiastic following.

This is the first ever privately owned Lotus Mk.7. In all its various guises, Lotus produced nearly 2700 of the Sevens before handing the model over to Caterham cars in 1973.

different form and was followed with a refreshingly revitalised enthusiasm. Ideal donor vehicles were the pre-war Austin Seven or Ford Ten, both of which were common and often cheap. Better still, they had separate chassis which allowed easy removal of the original bodywork and replacement of such with a shape very much more sporting. Styling was hardly the keyword with such designs as most builders kept their body building efforts simple and their materials usage to a minimum. What mattered was that the spartan machine had its priorities geared towards performance and so provided a refreshingly good drive. Here lay the origins of today's performance roadsters.

One such special builder was Colin Chapman. Late in 1947 he stripped an Austin Seven of its body, reinforced its chassis with box members and added a very simple plywood and aluminium shape that gave it the right to be called a sports car. Its name was the Lotus and Chapman was soon racing it with much success.

Another special, the Lotus Mk 2, followed before efforts were made to build more than one all-alloy bodied Mk 3 racer, again Austin Seven based. These attempts weren't entirely successful but, just as fledgling kit car manufacturers do today, Chapman persisted. Still working only part-time on his cars, he gained permission to use the stables behind his father's pub in Hornsey, North London, and in January 1952 formed Lotus Engineering. The 'production' model at the time was the Lotus Mk 4, a basic chariot using Ford 1172cc power in its modified Austin Seven chassis.

For whatever reason, there wasn't a Lotus Mk 5, so work soon progressed on to the Mk 6, and little could Chapman have realised what a huge impact the little car would have on sports car design for years hence. In this spaceframe chassised, Ford powered road/racer were the pure origins of the whole breed of cars described in this book, projectiles from the Lotus and Caterham Seven onwards which have been built in their thousands and given many generations of enthusiasts the ultimate pleasure and special thrills of 'real' sports car driving.

With the Mk 6, Lotus Engineering became rather more serious as a car manufacturer. Competition success came quickly but whether you intended your car for race or road use, you had to build it yourself from a kit, sourcing your own engine and running gear. A completed example could be roadworthy for around £400 and between 1952 and 1955 over 100 Mk 6's were built and supplied. Lotus was thriving and it was perhaps surprising that it took until 1957 for the famous Mk 7 to appear.

Of course, the early Lotuses were not alone in their spartan, minimalism charge towards cheap motoring thrills. Other well known names of the early 1950s were Lester, Turner, Cooper, Dellow, HRG and Elva, all of whom created and developed similarly basic performance roadsters. Indeed, if you wanted to build your own '50s equivalent of the 1990s kit car, there were many, many options from which to choose.

But it was the Lotus Seven which really sealed the future of the 'bare necessity' breed. Introduced in 1957, the little hotshot gained an awesome reputation over the years, and Lotus produced nearly 2700 examples (including the restyled Mk 4 version) before passing production rights to Caterham Cars in 1973. Other well known marques attempted to dent the Seven's tearaway ego, with models like the Ginetta G2 and Marcos GT, but they enjoyed little serious impact.

Announced in 1957 at around the same time as the Seven, the G2 looked very similar to the Lotus Six and employed a very similar construction: spaceframe chassis, stressed aluminium body, independent front suspension with split axle, a live rear axle and Ford 10 1172cc power. Around 100 examples were built between 1958 and the end of 1960, but the car never gained the lovable notoriety of the all-conquering Seven. Nor did 1959's Marcos GT, which was specifically created to do battle with the Lotus. This one had all-enveloping bodywork constructed as a wooden (yes!) monocoque and was naturally powered by Ford. But although the GT became a successful racer, its improved aerodynamics had little impact on the sales success of the Seven.

There wasn't then, and there never really has been ever since, any performance roadster to quite match the pure spirit, sparkling responses and relentless desirability of the Seven. Whatever the weather, there'll always be an endless stream of enthusiasts wanting to experience the thrill of a quite magical motor car.

And, as this book shows with its in-depth study of a wide range of minimalist chariots trying to chip away at the Seven block, there'll always be available a very capable variety of marques inspired by one of sports motoring's all-time greats. The immense popularity of such outlandish, functional automotive achievers shows no signs of relenting.

Lotus wasn't the only company producing stripped out two seaters, as this recently restored Ginetta G2 clearly demonstrates.

Chapter 2
Caterham 7

A Brief History

There isn't a pressing need to go through Caterham's history in detail yet again. It must be the best-documented evolution in the history of any current British manufacturer (if the reader accepts that Lotus hasn't been exactly British for a while). The Lotus and Caterham enthusiast already knows about Colin Chapman's development of the Lotus Mk.7 and its eventual move to the Caterham stable.

However, surprising though it may seem, there are some unfortunate folk out there who might not be familiar with the story behind the charming childhood and adolescence of the Seven – it wasn't a spoilt child by any means. One might even accuse its parents of a little neglect but the charismatic little machine made good in the end, didn't it? So it might just be worth going through the main facts, just to set the scene for the rest of this book and to demonstrate how the Lotus was indeed the *original* Seven. There's not a hint of snobbery about this assertion, it's just the plain truth.

Reprinted for the third time in 1993, Jeremy Coulter's book: *The Lotus And Caterham Sevens*, published by Motor Racing Publications, is a concise and comprehensive story of the car's development and its improbable history. From this book come the

Spiritual predecessor to the current crop of performance roadsters, this particular Lotus 7 was the very first privately owned car to hit the road.

most pertinent facts about the Seven's lineage. The legend is really a two-part story. Its first half concerns the car's life at the hands of creators, Lotus, and the second half is the contemporary story of its more recent guardians, Caterham Cars.

One of the fascinating little snippets to come from the history of the Lotus is that it was really the second Seven designed by Chapman. The first version was a one-off which was finally sold part-complete to the private customer for whom it had been designed. Several successive model number designations were built before the small, Hornsey-based company produced the official Series 1 Seven in 1957. The prototype had been available to the press the previous year and was very well received, its Ford 100E 1172cc sidevalve engine and three-speed manual gearbox permitting up to 80.4mph and 0-60 in 16.2 seconds!

This Seven was a hybrid of design concepts used in other Chapman inventions. It had a multi-tubular 18-gauge steel spaceframe chassis, diverging from the Six's use of twin main rails, but there was additional stiffening from riveted alloy sheets on the transmission tunnel and floor sections. This pretty aluminium-bodied and cycle-winged shape was very similar to that of today's Caterham but obviously much of the mechanical donor equipment was taken from production cars of that particular era.

Lotus' £536 kit (not subject to Purchase Tax) included all specially made parts as new, right up to the Ford engine and gearbox. For today's kit car manufacturers, kits such as that are right at the top end of the options list usually, as few customers can

The Lotus Seven quickly established an enviable reputation both with road and track users. Here a Seven charges down the Santa Pod straight in 1967.

afford such a specification or brand new parts. Interestingly, the Mk.7 Series 1 was also sold as a complete car at £1036 including Purchase Tax. Buyers started to queue, especially the amateur racing fraternity at the 750MC, but kit deliveries didn't start in earnest until 1958.

Wildly optimistic delivery promises, non-availability of parts and slow productionising of the Seven kit showed that Lotus didn't move right into smooth, effortless manufacturing. Their salubrious early premises were evidence of that. Having quoted a 'ready to go price' (inclusive of Purchase Tax) for the first Sevens, Jeremy Coulter's book also reports that the Inland Revenue inspectors were "just waiting for Lotus to overstep the mark and offer a car [kit] that was too fully assembled." They would then have been able to charge Purchase Tax.

The Seven boasted outrageously light weight and high power-to-weight ratio but it had a long way to go before it could be regarded as a near-practical proposition. It had poor quality weather gear, no wipers, fixed front cycle wings which didn't turn left to right with the steered wheels and it was claimed by observers that the styling was old-fashioned even then. Out on the race track, an early understanding of aerodynamics had already created some stunningly smooth, enclosed car shapes, such as the Lotus 11. The Seven's chassis in fact owed more to the Eleven than to the Six. Its front suspension was related to that of the Lotus Twelve single-seat Formula Two car. A mongrel with a real racing heritage.

Apparently, the very indeterminate regulations relating to kit cars meant that the Sevens could not be supplied with a build-up manual. As ever, the rules regarding kits were far from clear and were mainly agreed upon via some off-the-record talks with the Revenue. The factory found various ways in which it was possible to get around the grey areas and keep the customers informed about the build process.

Below: As an agent for Lotus, Caterham's Graham Nearn poses beside Patrick McGoohan and the Lotus Seven made famous by the cult TV series, The Prisoner. Bottom: Graham Nearn poses with Jools Holland and a 'replica' of KAR 120C in 1987.

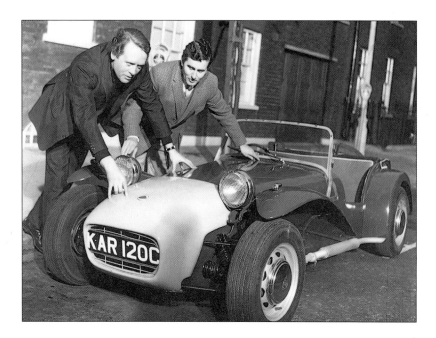

1958 was the Seven's first big year with around 100 units leaving the tiny London factory. Race competitors and other Seven owners around the country were already modifying the car for go-faster performance. DeDion rear suspension, alternative front suspensions and even 1098cc Coventry Climax engines were grafted in for better output. Not wishing to be left behind in all of this, the factory created its own Coventry Climax-powered evolutionary model and called it the Super Seven. The existing Ford-powered version was renamed Seven F.

At the same time, Lotus was trying to develop the GRP monocoque Elite coupe but with little luck as it was such a complex and pioneering project. The Sevens started to pull in fairly serious money. Straight away it looked like the Hornsey site was too small and Lotus was on the up and up.

In 1960, after around 250 Series One Seven Fs and Super Sevens had been produced, the long-running Series Two took over. Lotus had started to take the car seriously and a lot of modifications and improvements were made over the next few years. This was all accelerated by the introduction of new engines from Ford and other new parts from Triumph, which proved to be ideal for the Seven. Coulter reports that kit preparation time at the factory eventually went from something like 60 hours per package down to 12 hours.

Plenty of attention was given to profitability and Lotus' better understanding of GRP moulding left the S2 with a GRP nosecone, GRP front cycle or flared wings and GRP rear wings. Rationalisation meant removal of the front and rear sheet alloy undertrays but a more extensive use of sheet inside the car and around the cockpit. Removal of some of the many chassis tubes and suspension changes also speeded and simplified the production process.

At the beginning of the S2 run, the basic F-specification 100E engine was joined by the Leyland A-Series units as optional standard power. They were soon both ousted in favour of the smaller 105E Anglia 997cc unit fitted with twin SU carburettors and a four-speed Ford gearbox. This version appeared in late 1960. Yet another special Super Seven run was announced when the 1340cc 109E-powered (and Cosworth-modified) S2 appeared late in 1961.

The world famous *Prisoner* Lotus Seven was in fact a 1965 S2 factory demonstrator (registered KAR 120C) with a Cosworth 1500cc engine. Although it was shown on each of the twenty episodes of the curiously ambiguous TV series, Lotus was not really doing much to push sales of the S2 Seven at that time. Other products such as the Grand Prix cars,

the Elans and various clubmans racers were the money makers, and the Seven, being built upstairs at the Cheshunt works, was already receiving less attention. Chapman was nothing if not ambitious.

In 1966, following the company's move to its new Hethel, Norfolk, works, it looked like the Seven was about to be dropped. The Elan S2 and the Europa were the focus of attention. This is where Graham Nearn, boss of Lotus' sole Seven concessionaire, Caterham Cars of Caterham Hill, Surrey, really made his mark. He ordered another batch of twenty kits to get the production process moving again and followed this up with a set of new ideas for making the Seven more popular and therefore a worthwhile proposition for Lotus.

A short-lived Series 3 Seven was announced in 1968 and became the Seven which would be most familiar to Caterham owners of today. Changes included a Ford Escort rear axle (with welded-on reinforcement), new Ford PCD front hubs, Ford X-flow 1600cc engines as standard (designated 225E), standard disc brakes up front, wider 13" diameter wheels/tyres and a general improvement on overall equipment specification. It was most definitely a move up-market. Caterham Cars can be credited for many of these tweaks.

Among the upgrades was the fitment of a Lotus 1600cc twin-cam engine into an S3 car. 1969 had been a healthy year, with around 200 S3s leaving the Hethel works and Caterham doing just about all the selling. A reinforced chassis for the torquey twin-cam SS was the icing on the cake. That was the last year of the classic Seven shape as Lotus then went on to produce the all-GRP bodied (and extremely ugly) S4 from 1970 through to 1973, when the Seven line at Hethel was finally closed.

In a way, that's when things really started to take

Below: Caterham's Graham Nearn (left) with Colin Chapman (right) at the official handing over ceremony in 1973. Caterham also took on the Lotus Seven Mk.4 (above) but quickly concentrated on the prettier Mk.3.

off. Having perceived the imminent demise of the Seven, Caterham's Graham Nearn put in a bid for the manufacturing rights for that model. He was successful, probably because his company knew as much about Sevens as just about anyone else, and the hand-over was made in 1973. Caterham weren't allowed to call the car a Lotus and the original Lotus badge was removed from Caterham examples. The name Seven still stuck, though, and the small Caterham concern went ahead with their quite impressive gamble.

Difficulty in sourcing new parts for production soon put an end to the hideous S4 version and

Arch Motors. They had been making the bronze-welded chassis for Lotus Sevens since the S2 programme and found no problem in reverting to the S3 jigs and supplying to Caterham instead of Hethel.

From then on, the already quick Lotus Seven started to get really quick and to go right up-market. It was still the essential kit car, with some fully completed models going abroad, but there was really very little meaningful opposition. Colin Chapman's pioneering work in suspension and handling had made the car a road and track flier and it had a head start over other vehicles seeking to do the same. Lotus' Elite and Elan kits had reinforced their experience at turning out cars that could be built up by amateur customers from basic or more comprehensive packages.

While the Caterham Seven styling has changed little over the years, the car has been continually fine-tuned.

Caterham had little choice but to move back in time to the S3 variant in 1974. The version that was adopted included a standard Lotus Big Valve Twin Cam 1600 engine and the reinforced chassis of the limited edition S3 SS twin-cam (plus some extra strengthening), which continued to be produced at

Having had most of the direct customer contact since they originally became sole concessionaires for the Seven in 1967, Caterham Cars knew a lot about the kind of Seven that would sell and that would establish a rock-solid performance reputation for the model. Now that they had achieved ownership of the Seven's production tooling and associated parts, with the contractually guaranteed help of the Lotus

Hethel factory, they could really start to motor.

After a couple of years, with the majority of Caterhams being factory-completed and exported with twin-cam units, it looked like the Lotus engines were running out. Some of the Caterhams received Vegantune versions of the 1600 TC but that supply also started to dwindle. It was back to a modified version of the OHV Ford Kent X-flow 1600, producing around 110bhp reliably. That was the Caterham Seven Sprint.

Other production refinements and changes continued throughout the 'seventies. There was a long-cockpit chassis option for taller drivers, and the 2000E Corsair gearboxes ran out, to be replaced by the Ford Escort Sport item. The Escort axles dried up right at the end of the decade, to be replaced by a Morris Marina/Ital version which was 30lbs lighter, still needing reinforcement. This meant a return to the standard Triumph front hubs and uprights as the wheel stud PCD was the same as the Ital's.

Caterham needed to keep its eyes open for new suppliers as and when non-factory parts supplies started to become unreliable or obsolete. Luckily, there was plenty of rear-drive equipment still available in those days, even if the original models themselves had disappeared.

An answer to the twin-cam engine drought came in 1983 when Cosworth Engineering told Caterham about their new 1600 BDR 16-valve TC. The first Caterham with this exciting new fitment appeared in 1984 and managed around 120mph with the 0-60 time down to just over five seconds. Not bad compared with the 17.8 seconds of the 1172cc S1 Seven F of 1957.

A little earlier, in 1982, the Seven celebrated 25 years in production (Caterham produced a Jubilee model to mark the occasion). The start of the 'eighties was actually the start of the kit car boom decade. It's interesting to note that the Seven had been around for at least twenty five years when many of today's other famous kit car manufacturers were just getting started. The 'eighties was also to see the start of the Seven clone trend, which persists to this day. In some respects, it is an indication of how ingenious and popular the original Seven had become.

Fears concerning the supplies of Ital live axles galvanised Caterham into action in the middle of the decade. There had to be a back-up Caterham rear suspension just in case axle supplies really fell away.

Caterham has always had a strong competition heritage. Here's a massively tyred Seven competing the 1978 Brighton Speed Trials.

Some Lotus Sevens had previously been fitted with high-specification deDion rear suspensions, usually for competition purposes. These combined live axle-type rear wheel location with a chassis-mounted differential. Less complex than an independent rear set-up but lighter on the unsprung weight than a live axle.

That theme was pursued by Caterham's Reg Price and Clive Roberts in their search for an alternative to the possibly doomed Ital version. Using the handy new Ford Sierra rear differential, the team produced a deDion rear axle and suspension prototype within a month of doing the drawings. A completed deDion Caterham was shown for the first time at the 1984 Motor Show in Birmingham. Emergency over, even if the cost was higher.

If the tuned 1600 Ford Kent engine was the Sprint, what on earth was the Super Sprint? It was, believe it or not, an even higher specification Kent. This time, it was taken out to 1700cc with the requisite alteration to ancillary equipment and returned a reputed 135bhp. Very nice, too. Cosworth applied the same big-bore philosophy to their BDR, in 1986, and that returned 170bhp as a consequence of the extra capacity.

With a 0-60 time of five seconds dead, the BDR-powered Caterham Seven HPC of 1986 was a lethal weapon in the wrong hands. In order to underline the importance of driving safety when behind the wheel of such a car, Caterham named the model after John Lyons' High Performance Course. Buyers were required to attend such a course before taking delivery of the Caterham HPC. It also made a good publicity piece for the magazines.

Light weight combined with impressive levels of power have always endowed the Caterham with phenomenal speed whether competing in hill climbs, sprints or traditional track events.

By all accounts, though, the course is still very worthwhile. The HPC may not have had the world's best top speed, due to fairly terrible aerodynamics, but it remained practically the fastest cross-country road rocket available and that took driving into new dimensions for most owners of production cars.

1986 was a record year for Caterham production and sales. The waiting list was long and the money rolled in. Thatcher's credit boom was reaching full swing. However, the cramped and ancient production facilities at Caterham Hill were no longer sufficient and, for the umpteenth time in its life, the Seven production 'line' was uprooted and moved to a new factory in October 1987. This was Caterham's new plant purchased at Crayford in Kent. A sales office and showroom maintained the geographical link with Caterham but everything else went to the impressively large premises in Kent.

This proved to be a completely worthwhile risk as just three years later, in 1990, Caterham production reached a massive 780 units in a year. Pretty impressive stuff. Purchasing director Andrew Noble reported that 60% of that year's production was for the UK market and most of the remainder went to Japan and to European destinations. There is no doubt that it is still the best-selling kit car of all time and seems to be retaining that title despite the relatively high price tag compared to other kits now widely available in the UK.

The early 'nineties saw new additions to all levels of performance in the Caterham range. In 1990, the company adopted the 2-litre Vauxhall twin-cam 16-

Caterham has had its fair share of important visitors. Here Sir Geoffrey Howe visits the company on it 25th anniversary. Below: The move to new manufacturing premises in 1987 was vital to the company's continued growth.

valve GTE engine for the HPC models, ousting the Cosworth unit. 165bhp, 0-60 in 4.9 and 126mph top end with unleaded fuel to boot. A clever move indeed.

Somewhere near the middle of the scale came the Rover 1400-powered Caterham K-Series model. This TC 16V version was primarily for the foreign complete car market and its multi-point fuel injection helped Caterham to offer a car which could comply with ever more stringent pollution rules in export destinations. Unbeknown to many, it was also the basis for the first LVTA Caterham, the first Seven to be fully approved for turn-key sale in the UK.

At the other end of the scale, the GTS was introduced in 1992. This offered kit builders the chance at a lower budget Caterham with a 1600 Kent pushrod engine and the Ital live axle. The rest of the model range, probably due to huge demand in the 'eighties, had become rather expensive. Somewhere along the line, Caterham's management of the Seven project had turned the car into a luxury item rather than cheap, tax-free transport for the impecunious club racer.

The Classic did a little to

Above: The new premises at Dartford were in sharp contrast to the previously cramped works in Caterham. Below: All basic Caterham kits are supplied as a panelled chassis with wings pre-fitted. Bottom: Demonstration chassis at the Stoneleigh kit car show.

redress the balance. Its initial purchase price was higher than the competition's, even if the specification was very comprehensive, and that's what allowed the increasing number of Seven clones to become quite popular. The latter appealed to the kind of customer that the original Seven might have appealed to back in the 'fifties.

Out at the lunatic fringe of performance, the Jonathan Palmer Evolution (JPE) limited edition model appeared in the same year as the Classic. Using a very interestingly modified Vauxhall engine and loads of lightweight, hi-tech materials, the JPE recorded a 0-60 run in 3.44 seconds. That got an entry in the *Guinness Book Of Records* as the fastest 0-60 for a production car. However, it wasn't actually available as a turn-key production car in the UK. Notwithstanding, foreign demand, notably from Japan, was strong enough to justify the manufacture of seventeen of these cars.

Caterham's most ambitious leap forward has been the Type Approval of two models for the UK and foreign markets. It's a complex business, as the company was already selling completed cars abroad, mostly to Japan, but the new LVTA rules have meant that the relevant Caterham models are more widely accepted by the stricter transport departments of the target countries.

First to meet the stringent tests for LVTA, as mentioned already, was the K-Series 1400cc Caterham fitted with the Rover four-cylinder twin-cam of the same name. That model became available in the UK in early 1993. It was followed by approval of the top-of-the-range HPC model in July of the same year, just in time for the new L-registration.

So, thirty-seven years after the inception of the S1 Seven by Lotus, Caterham had nurtured the orphan to adulthood. Judging by the attitude at the Crayford works, though, the Seven is still young and there's a long way to go before all the improvements that can be thought of are actually tried out. What will the next few decades hold?

Caterham Cars Today

Because of its enormous head start over other current production kit cars, the Caterham Seven still finds itself in a position of market strength. Sales figures for 1993 showed that the company moved around 700 units per year but the difference these days is that they sell better abroad than they do in the UK. That's pretty amazing as export models are sold complete and cost somewhere in the region of £25,000 a piece in Japan, according to Andrew Noble, one of the company directors. In the same year Caterham received the Queen's Award for Export, with 55% of output leaving the country.

There seems little doubt that the company has quite safely survived the recent recession and is now gaining headway yet again under the guidance of Graham Nearn and a growing number of in-house experts. A visit to the premises in Crayford gives a good idea as to the size of the operation. The showroom and sales department in Caterham occupies a new but modestly sized ground floor office

Above: Just some of the pre-dispatch assembly work being done on a typical Caterham kit. Below: This car is being prepared for the Caterham one-make race series.

space and may be a little misleading in terms of size.

There's nothing bright and gaudy about the frontage of the Crayford works. A small Caterham Cars sign greets the visitor, who is left in no doubt as to the purpose of the premises. There are always several completed Sevens outside the front of the office entrance to prove that you've arrived at the right place. In fact, the rather anonymous office effectively hides the imposing size of the factory areas to its rear and side. No less than 30,000 square feet are available in the main Unit 2 and

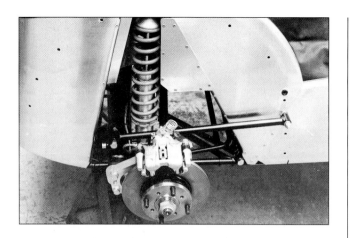

Top: Rear disc conversion one of the many options available. Above: Marina/Ital live axles after modification.

another 20,000 square feet in the adjoining Unit 3. The latter is mainly for storage and for receipt and despatch of goods.

A spacious reception area greets the customer and straight ahead, opposite the entrance, is a parts counter with many specific Caterham components on display. Offices are to be found to the left and right but a brief walk brings you out into the bright and spacious main workshop and stores building. It's a far cry from the run-down old factory at Caterham and, with its tidy central walkway and neat assembly bays lined up along the walls, it is just how a quality hand-made car production line should be.

There are no hi-tech conveyor belts or overhead chassis/body support hooks. The chassis being prepared as kits or as completed cars are to be found on axle stands or on trestles, each with one or two of the assembly staff carefully working around it. Andrew Noble went through the basic process with us and it gives some idea of why the main works can remain so tidy and ordered.

In effect, the main processes involved in the manufacture of a Seven or the collation of a Seven kit haven't really changed much over the years. Arch Motors still produce the various chassis, with that time-honoured bronze welding technique, so there's practically no fabrication at all done at the Caterham works. For those unfamiliar with the technique, bronze welding isn't run of the mill welding. No dramatic showers of sparks and noisy, crackling electric machines.

It's actually more like soldering. A quiet but intensely hot gas flame is used to heat up chassis member joins and a hand-held, bronze-based rod is melted neatly into the joint. It's immensely strong and practitioners of the art will say that the steel tubes themselves will break before the bronze-welded joint. Because the chassis still use stressed aluminium sheet as part of their structure, much of this is also done before the chassis are delivered to Crayford. Needless to say, all chassis are given rust-resistant finishes before panelling.

GRP mouldings, offered with a final gel coat colour and forming the nosecone, cycle or clamshell wings, rear arches etc., are produced by Ford Composites or Fibresports. There's nothing new about

Below: More basic models have a traditional lower wishbone with upper arm and anti-roll bar doubling as part of the top 'wishbone'. Bottom: Double wishbone with anti-roll bar for DeDion cars.

the laminating techniques for standard specification bodywork, either. The layers of mat are hand-rolled in the mould for careful resin impregnation.

One of the big advantages that the company has is that the moulding sub-contractors do have different sets of moulds for different gel coat colours. This means that the quality of each set of mouldings is more consistent, with less likelihood of pigment contamination which can sometimes be caused when one set of moulds is used for all gel colour options. If you want something even more traditional than this, then you could always opt for the complete alloy body Seven re-introduced in 1993 as an option by Caterham. Rolling and shaping alloy to these shapes is certainly still a craftsman's task. Price on application!

Oxted Trimming of Surrey still supply the trim and weather gear for the whole range and they do an extremely professional job of it. Like many of Caterham's suppliers, they have been doing it for a number of years and Sevens are probably their biggest business. When a company has a good list of suppliers who get large quantities of orders on a regular basis, mainly from the one client, their reliability tends to improve a great deal.

It's an unfortunate fact that some kit car companies suffer from indifferent quality accessories as they are only able to order special components in small quantities. The supplier can't become an expert at producing that tonneau, casting or fabrication as

volume is too low.

Because so much of the Caterham Seven is shipped in from outside, the Unit 2 stores and assembly plant stays much tidier than a factory which covers all aspects of kit manufacture under one roof. Resin fumes, sticky lumps of half-cured mat, steel filings, swarf, welding smoke, industrial noise and horrible second-hand car bits are all absent from the Crayford plant. It's practically assembly and stores only. A very smooth operation.

Various chassis, in left or right hand drive guises,

Two of Caterham's lessor known engine options. Above: Ford BDR twin-cam engines are still to be found at the factory. Below: Vegantune twin-cam power is even less common. Both loads of fun.

Caterham's store rooms clearly illustrate the company's huge size.

empire. That breaks down to around seven engineers, six stores staff, four at the parts counter, four managers, two receptionists, two book-keepers, one accountant, four directors, one M.D. and somewhere in the region of twenty shop floor workers. At the 5000 sq. ft. Caterham sales office, there's the sales manager, three salesmen and two administrators. In all, about fifteen of these staff members own Sevens!

How traumatic was the move from Caterham to Crayford? "Most of the staff came along with us," says Andrew Noble. "We would have loved to build a factory at Caterham, though." At the end of the day, However, there was little alternative to a move to Crayford. It had been used by a different company previously and Caterham went into the new place and designed all of the internal partitioning to suit the purposes in hand.

Running parallel to the assembly lines in Unit 2, the stores take up a good deal of space, even though the components are all carefully labelled and stowed militarily on uniform shelving. Here's the evidence of a large turnover and substantial buying power. Remember that there are perhaps an additional 300 Caterham kits in circulation in the UK every year and all of the previous year's buyers could be in the market for spares or upgrades as with any other car.

are parked up against the two longer walls of Unit 2 and there's a continuous buzz of activity around many of these body/chassis units. Each is accompanied by a clipboard detailing the specification of the car. This must be strictly adhered to in order to avoid the kind of problem that Lotus used to have when demand outstripped supply and manpower availability. It was not uncommon, in the early days, for Lotus customers to be given the wrong parts or even the wrong kit on the hectic Friday collection day.

One of the more noticeable aspects of Caterham's car building staff is that they generally appear to be very absorbed in what they are doing. No scowling groups of alienated grease monkeys keeping a lookout for the boss. This is, at the risk of using cliches, a stable of enthusiasts and several of the assemblers are also Caterham or Lotus owners.

Purchasing director Andrew Noble claims a full-time staff of approximately sixty for the Caterham

There's an unrivalled stockpile of beautifully made alloy castings for gearbox conversions, exhausts with integral silencers/catalytic converters, brake, fuel and safety parts, trim and seats, and suspension parts for different models. It's all there in large quantities and there's a lot of computing work done to keep tabs on the whole lot and to ensure re-ordering as and when necessary.

Even the lowliest CKD Classic kit is pretty comprehensive – that's part of the reason why Caterham's cars are more expensive than alternative clones. As a consequence, the spares stocks have to be pretty enormous. 700 cars in a year means 3500 wheels/tyres, 2800 coil-over shock absorbers, 700 engines, 700 gearboxes, 700 wiring looms, sets of instruments, hoods, trim kits, carpet sets, hubs, uprights, axles, differentials, deDion tubes, radiators etc. etc. Sevens may be small but they are packed to the hilt with equipment and the advent of more complex engines means more complex componentry to go with them.

A small research and development shop in Unit 2 houses several race and ex-race cars, along with

interesting one-offs and performance ideas that may come in handy for the UK or foreign Caterham racing series. More about those later. It's small design and build shops like this which can give rise to the smallest chassis refinements or to a vehicle such as the JPE, with its record-breaking acceleration. One of its occupants actually won a 24-hour race in America, much to the surprise of the massive V8s against which the 2-litre HPC was competing.

Next door, the relatively quiet Unit 3 is yet another indication of the amount of work being undertaken on a daily basis at Caterham Cars. Vertical stacks of chassis reach skyward, accompanied by forests of wheels, tyres and wooden crates which contain what could be the world's very last significant stocks of new Ford Kent X-flow 1600 engines.

There is very little activity in this unit and it's a strangely awe-inspiring experience to stroll past the stacks of new engines and other performance parts just waiting to be turned into some of the world's quickest cars. Somewhere, some customer in Newcastle, Tokyo or Berlin is going to get this or that chassis with this or that engine, and it will undoubtedly redefine their expectations of a sports cars.

Upstairs in the same unit, orderly piles of parts stacked on pallets await delivery to their respective UK customers. These are the non chassis/body kit parts and

identifying tags tell the transport staff where to take each package. No-one collects a Caterham from the works these days. They all get delivered. It's just that 350-odd UK customers turning up at the factory would be a daunting task for the staff, especially if everyone wanted a tour of the factory and a technical chat each time...

Because Caterham Cars has such a long history of exporting Sevens to the rest of the world, the staff have put together a pretty impressive team of agents,

Above: Caterham Classic is the company's budget model and is powered by a standard 1600cc Ford X-flow engine with decent single carburettor.

as well as a good stock of knowledge concerning the regulations affecting car specification, taxation and transportation to various countries. Agencies extend as far and wide as Switzerland and Singapore, America and Australia, Japan and Canada, the Arabian Gulf and Macau. There are five agents in the UK, all of whom can help local customers with their official post-build safety check and supply of new parts.

Substantial investments have been made to get the cars approved for turn-key sale in each country but the length of time taken to get this far has obviously helped to spread the cost. Different companies wishing to compete on the same terms would have to plough an awful lot of money into getting all the necessary paperwork done over a short time span – even if the car in question was up to the job.

How complex is it? "Well," reflects Andrew, with a rather wry expression on his face, "Singapore, for instance, has a 200% import tax. The government will buy back your car after eight years, paying the owner 80% of its new price at the time. That is in order to stabilise the number of cars in the country. It's OK unless your car actually appreciates in value over the years. The United States and Australia charge a 40% import tax and we have to pay particular attention to

Classic interior will not normally feature the full set of instruments here but trim set is quite adequate. Simply Classic!

the necessary public liability insurance." A minefield to say the least.

"In Japan, they're absolutely crazy about Caterhams, even though they're expensive out there. When I visited the country, I was chauffeured around like a king! They have much greater purchasing power because much of the population rents accommodation. House prices are so high that not many are able to buy their own. That gives them a lot more disposable income as they are not usually saddled with a mortgage."

Because exports of completed cars account for over 50% of total unit output, this puts Caterham in the unique position of being the only kit car manufacturer producing more turn-key cars than kits. That doesn't necessarily mean that the kit-form Seven is to die a death in favour of the high-budget drive-away versions. The home market is still substantial and is still primarily reliant on the amateur kit builder.

As far as that amateur constructor is concerned, the image of the Seven has changed diametrically since the days when it was a kit of parts for the aspiring track racer. When Lotus was first in the business of selling Seven kits, customers really were inclined to be robust car makers. Not many people complained when something didn't fit, they fixed it. There were various manufacturing inconsistencies, right down to chassis members appearing in different places. The Lotus kit assemblers took each car at face value and coerced all the ancillary components for the best fit. The customer had to do much the same.

Evolution is something of which the Seven has not been shy. When a car has been around for that many years – and not many current models have – the manufacturer can't help but improve it. The Seven has developed into a state-of-the-art kit of parts – something to which other quality manufacturers can refer as a yardstick.

Instead of giving the customer a temptation to undertake home-made conversions, the company has done much to improve conformity by assuring that all of the kits sent out have a great deal of the difficult work done – and all of the necessary parts supplied in them, including new engines. A list of seven different road-going kits and three race kits will also do much to stop adventurous amateurs from creating one-off nightmares in an attempt to get a more suitable car. Add to this an excellent and very hefty build manual covering all models and there are the foundations for the ultimately buildable, quality kit.

Any number of more subjective assumptions also seem to arise as explanations for Caterham's transformation of the Seven into a high-budget, high-quality machine. For a start, the new Caterham owner can think of him or herself as being the latest

Above: 1700cc Super Sprint looks the part and is powered by the excellent tuned X-flow engine with twin Webers (below). Left: Standard interior still pretty basic.

in a line of red-blooded performance motoring enthusiasts dating back to the very earliest of Chapman's followers. There's an odd feeling associated with driving a car which brings real heritage with it. Something you can't get from an Escort or an Astra. Obviously, feeling that you've put your own effort into the construction of the vehicle also infers a kind of baptism.

What about the new sector of Caterham owners in the UK? Those who want the LVTA K-Series or HPC models. Will there be a new rash of 'uninformed' Seven drivers, separated from the existing self-build hard core? Probably not. Caterham has gone ahead with the LVTA testing of two models to assist with exports more than anything else. It looks like the kind of people who will buy a Seven in the UK are mostly those who are willing and able to put it together. Making the cars available as higher-priced complete vehicles hasn't suddenly doubled sales overnight.

There will be those who are equally enthusiastic about the cars as the amateur builders have been for decades but have neither the time, the ability, the volition nor the space to put one together. There isn't that great a penalty really, as the difference between the kit and complete car prices has been kept to a practical minimum. It might seem just a little too much for the amateur build enthusiast who knows that it really won't take that long to put the Caterham together these days. For the customer whose time is more important than money, there are now options.

It was really the boom 'eighties which set Caterham apart from other kit car manufacturers. The kit buying public, boosted by loads of credit

Graham Nearn with Sir Graham Day, chairman of The Rover Group, in one of the new Rover K-Series engined cars.

availability, turned towards Caterham as the mother of all kits. That's when they started getting seriously aloof from the rest of the field. Admittedly, they had a lot to feel superior about – customer satisfaction being one of the big features of the marque. They were rarely to be seen in the pages of the popular kit car magazines and although the entire kit car trade was booming, they were already way ahead.

Because the rest were advertising relatively sparse kits compared with the Caterham specification, the Sevens seemed to be in a different price bracket. Needless to say, builders buying other alternatives quite regularly spent Caterham money in the end, even if the price lists did say that they could get their kit for under £2000.

Graham Nearn was (and still is) chairman of the Specialist Car Manufacturer's Group, affiliated to the Society of Motor Manufacturers and Traders. This small group of kit car companies sought to promote higher standards of design and build in kit cars, thereby distancing themselves from lesser companies, some of whom were undoubtedly out for cynical gain alone. The group also gave the kit car manufacturers a voice in the crowd of mainstream manufacturers and a unified organisation which the government agencies could identify.

Alas, the development budgets and engineering know-how which were precursors to SCMG membership precluded most other manufacturers from joining. Unfortunately, this meant that some very competent kits were not able to attain membership. It gave the SCMG a somewhat elitist image and restricted its growth. Mr. and Mrs. Public carried on buying kits that were more affordable. Caterham still managed high sales improvements until the slump at the end of the 'eighties and the beginning of the 'nineties. "UK demand declined by 20% in the recession," remembers Andrew Noble. Caterham put in a bit more effort to appeal to the lower budget end of the market with their Classic kit.

With demand currently picking up again in the UK, it is obvious that Caterham can't be accused of standing still in relation to market forces. "We're always working at improving the cars," claims Andrew. "Everyone who works here wants to make the car better. Without improving things, you achieve nothing. That's why the light at the end of the tunnel always seems to be moving further away." That's presumably a reference to new technology and better mechanical parts constantly appearing on the market.

Even though the updated S3 Seven look is still retained, giving the Caterham that all-important visual conformity, things 'under the bonnet' are forever changing. It would probably be untrue to say that the Seven has 'made it'. Judging by the enthusiasm of customers and staff, the car is still in its infancy and potential refinements are infinite in nearly every price bracket.

With the uncompromising goals of performance, handling and buildability the main inspirations behind development work, the company isn't restricting itself to the myriad half-measures that the mainstream car manufacturer must put up with. It doesn't have to be practical, it doesn't need four seats, ABS brakes, air-conditioning, doors or electric windows – it just needs to be quick, quicker, quickest!

On the subject of quick, what about those racing series? Are Caterhams reduced to the status of weekend playthings to be polished by the ex-yuppie set? Chapman intended his Seven to be a car that a budget-minded owner could commute with during the week and race with at the weekend, without horrendous repair bills. Well, there's still no shortage of people wishing to race their Caterhams, both in this country and abroad.

In the UK, there are currently three racing classes solely for Caterhams, run in conjunction with the BRSCC and incorporating the relevant RACMSA regulations. At the top of the price and specification league is the Vecta/Caterham/Vauxhall Championship. Out 'n' out racers using 'sealed' (same specification) Vauxhall twin cams and twin 48 Webers compete in the Class A event to show each other what driving skill can achieve rather than just budget differences.

The Caterham Seven Challenge caters for the lower budget racers and again offers strict controls on engine output for extra competitiveness. Class B of this series incorporates cars with the 1600 or 1700cc X-flow engines, live axle or deDion rear ends and a limit of 155bhp. The Class C category incorporates the 1600 GT Sprint and the K-Series cars using the unique Super K 130bhp specification agreed between Rover and Caterham for the 1400cc unit. This is the most economical class to compete in and is an ideal starting point in motorsport.

HPC and K-Series races for Caterhams have been established in France but Andrew Noble is particularly pleased about the Japanese venture. "We have the

Above: The Caterham K-series was the company's first car to be sold fully built having obtained LVTA. Below: More powerful K- series Supersport engine specially developed by Rover.

only one-make series to be held in Japan featuring non-Japanese cars." That must have been a political triumph at the negotiating table. It also comes from a very good relationship with the Japanese agent, Kiwa Trading Company of Tokyo.

It's a little difficult not to sound somewhat partisan when describing Caterham's kits and its approach to kit building. It's the kind of operation that many a kit car manufacturer might hold up as a dream goal for the future. Admittedly, the Lotus connection has given the Caterham not only the air of being the original but the pedigree to go with it.

That's not the whole story, though. Plenty of well-bred British sports cars have fallen by the wayside even though the product was good. The unending development and modernisation done by Caterham, as well as the flexibility of selling a car in kit form, seem to have assured the Seven's future for a good while yet.

Current Models

Depending upon which piece of Caterham literature the enthusiast might read, or which member of staff is consulted, or which new invention has just been incorporated, it's a little difficult to pin down just which kits Caterham is currently offering. The company's official *Information Price Guide and Order Form* tells us that there are seven kit packages (all upgradeable to the higher 'Component Form' specification at a uniform £1500 inclusive), two race car kits and two fully built cars on offer.

These are the 1600 Classic (84bhp, four-speed with live axle), the 1600 Classic SE (100bhp, four-speed with live axle), the 1700 Classic SE (135bhp, four-speed with live axle), the 1600 Sprint (100bhp, five-speed with deDion axle), the 1400 K-Series (110bhp, five-speed with deDion axle), the 1700 Super Sprint (135bhp, five-speed with deDion axle), the 2000 HPC (165bhp, five-speed with deDion axle), the Class C 1400 K-Series Race (110bhp), the 2000 Vauxhall/Caterham Challenge Race, the fully built 1400 K-Series (110bhp, five-speed with deDion axle) and the fully built 2000 HPC (165bhp, five-speed with deDion axle).

It can be a little confusing for the absolute newcomer but the sales staff are very well equipped to explain the ins and outs of different specifications in the range. There will be something there for the mildest to wildest sports driving enthusiast.

A million refinements notwithstanding, the Super Seven models are all based around much the same chassis concept as the early Lotus. This is primarily a lightweight, multi-tubular spaceframe using a combination of (mainly round section) steel tubes attached to each other using traditional bronze welding techniques.

The fact that the chassis is lightweight doesn't infer that it is therefore weak. Some of the Lotus chassis did take the lightweight philosophy to the extreme but Caterham have seen to it that the standard and the long-cockpit chassis are designed for proper road use, not just for the track. Chapman was very good at inventing steel tube structures in such a way as to achieve maximum stiffness with minimum materials. This has always been an essential requirement for small-capacity, quick cars. It's how owners are able to be competitive in races without spending fortunes on bags of extra horsepower from really exotic engines.

Extensive triangulation of the chassis

Below: K-series looks the business in the Caterham's engine bay. Bottom: This car features the optional cycle front wings.

Above: Leather seats are superb but expensive option. Below: Soft top works well.

framework has lead to beam and torsional stiffness in the front and rear bulkhead areas, the side rails and the transmission tunnel. The inner parts of the cockpit area and the outer tub are extensively skinned in specially riveted aluminium sheet to further improve stiffness. The trick is to design all the engine, gearbox and suspension load-bearing members so that the stresses are efficiently channelled in to the very strongest parts of the structure. This minimises chassis flex and breakages. When a chassis is stiff, suspension geometries can be very accurately calculated for the best possible roadholding. Caterham has become a master at this, especially with its extensive race expertise.

Chassis variations have been designed to accept the (reinforced Ital/Marina) live axle or the deDion rear suspensions. They are different because the loads imparted by a live axle are transmitted through the lower A-frame and the single radius rod each side. The axle casing itself is also subjected to torque reaction from acceleration, deceleration and braking.

Although a deDion rear end is like a lightweight live axle, it is subtly different in that the torque reaction from acceleration and deceleration is transmitted into the chassis via the separate Sierra differential. Special chassis tubes were designed to properly support the differential at the rear end of the transmission tunnel. Again, we find that the deDion tube is located with two upper radius rods and a lower A-arm.

The A-arm in question has its apex to the rear, at the centre of the lower part of the tube or the live axle differential housing. Its wide-based front bushes meet the lower part of the chassis so that the overall rear geometry is as free as possible of arc conflicts. In this way the A-arm does the job of a pair of lower radius rods and a Panhard rod, but with fewer bushes, fewer tubes and less weight. Very fiendish and quite competent, but not necessarily the best live axle location to be found in a kit car. Twin coil-over shock absorbers and disc or drum brakes complete the back end suspension.

A short, specially made propshaft joins the differential or axle to a Ford four or five-speed gearbox which, via several superb conversion kits, is

Above: Caterham HPC is the company's top spec kit option using the tuned Vauxhall 2-litre twin-cam to provide ample power (below).

mounted to Caterham's selection of engines. No problems about sourcing bits as the Seven kits contain everything needed. The customer might pay extra for some of the assembly work to be undertaken by the factory in advance of delivery, hence the popular Component Form packages.

Traditionally, the Seven's front suspension involves Triumph Spitfire uprights and hubs but development has meant that most of it is specially made for Caterham these days. Especially as front set-ups and brakes are subject to wide variations in customer demand.

In general, the live-axled cars will be fitted with a pair of front lower wishbones working in unison with single upper links. An upper anti-roll bar stiffens the suspension in roll but also acts as triangulation for the upper arms each side, effectively creating upper wishbones. In recent years, though, Caterham developed a complete upper wishbone for the deDion cars, to give better levels of castor adjustment at the top end of the range. The upper anti-roll bar is still featured on these cars, with a clever new knuckle-joint linkage each side at the wishbone ends.

Again, a selection of different coil-over shocks, brake discs and calipers is available depending upon the car's intended purpose. A specially made steering rack and column linkage rounds off the assembly, which provides a driving feel second to none. Drivers experiencing this will never see that awful invention, front wheel drive, in the same light again!

Massive amounts of development work have gone into accumulating all of the components necessary for neat and tidy engine and gearbox fitment under the bonnet, including all of the other ancillaries that couldn't possibly be fitted if taken straight from a donor car. Because of Caterham's

relatively massive buying power and their in-house design facilities, it has been possible for them to manufacture special induction and injection ancillaries, carburettor manifolds, wiring looms, pedal boxes, radiators, tubes, pipes, hoses, mounts etc. Some of this has been done with the collusion of the engine manufacturers themselves. Andrew Noble reports that Rover have been particularly obliging with developments for the K-Series car.

As the builder inevitably discovers, there's more than just a knack when it comes to cramming a powerful engine into a small and low-level engine bay. Sumps need to be shallow, gear levers need to appear at the correct places, exhausts, carburettors, filters and radiator fans all have to clear chassis members and bodywork. Not only that, all of the relevant parts have to be readily available off the shelf at the factory and priced reasonably. It's no good saying that the distributor from the limited edition 1908 version of such and such a donor car is just the job. No-one will be able to get one in good condition and maintenance parts will be impossible to find. An impressive juggling act by Caterham there.

Beautifully made stainless side exit and full length exhaust systems feature in the Caterham range. They can be supplied with or without catalytic converter – an important point for foreign destinations. Heat shields are made to help protect the occupants from scalded hands or legs. Because of the limited ground clearance, the silencers are to be found at the side of the main body, not underneath.

Most customers opt for a comprehensive range of instruments fitted into the alloy dash panel at the factory. The company has invested in excellent purpose-built wiring looms to bring together all of the various engines, after-market instruments, special alarm systems, heated windscreen options and ancillary controls. No column stalks are used but excellent line-of sight main gauges and a comprehensive array of minor gauges accompany the toggle switches on most Seven dashboards.

What about the furniture? Again, that depends on how much you want to spend. The S-type interior trim kit offers body-hugging seats, leather trim and Wilton carpet at a high budget. You could go for basic squab seats and lower specification trim and carpets – especially as this is the kind of car that is destined to get wet more than once in its life! Again, there has been a great deal of attention paid to getting these components cut and finished for a very accurate fit.

Things like this are of paramount

Caterham's £33,000+ JPE was the company's attempt to produce the fastest accelerating car in the world!

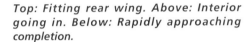

Top: Fitting rear wing. Above: Interior going in. Below: Rapidly approaching completion.

Which Kit? *magazine built a Classic kit in less than seven days. Top: Complete kit unloaded from the lorry. Above: Assembling the front suspension.*

importance when a factory has to build up the majority of its cars in-house. The assemblers can't be left to design each individual interior because the fit varies. Economics dictates that it has to be quicker and more certain than that. The interior is generally the least satisfactory part of many kit cars and amateur builders around the country will gladly relate nightmare stories about the effort needed to get their car looking right. All too often, the trim and weather gear can be a let-down, compromising a kit car's general appearance. It's another example of the Caterham preference for assured homogeneity in their kits.

In a sensible move to reduce the overall build budget, the Super Seven is available with a standard alloy-finish central body and self-coloured GRP

Which Kit?*'s Caterham Classic after just seven days!*

components such as the nose, wings and rear arches. The builder needn't spend out on a paint job at all. There are obviously factory paint options and many of the demonstrators get an overall metallic paint finish to very good effect.

If the car is purchased in Caterham's Complete Kit (CKD) form, the factory claims a seventy hour build time on average. These are in fact the most basic kit packages sold by Caterham but actually include all that you need to finish the car. They come with the bodywork, windscreen assembly, fuel tank, pedals, instruments, wiring and plumbing already fitted.

For an inclusive charge of £1000 per kit, you can upgrade to the Component Form vehicle with an estimated 20 hours of work for completion. Simple assembly work, requiring no special tools, might be properly finished in a weekend for the car builder who hasn't much spare time.

If it is the customer's intention to enter one of the Caterham one-make race series, then the staff will advise on the appropriate kit for the particular series favoured. There are race kits built specifically for the 1400 K-Series, GTS and HPC 2-litre models, so there's no shortage of choice. Special springs, shocks, brakes, dry sump equipment and cooling parts? It's all there for the right money.

Just how expensive are the Caterhams? Right at the bottom of the 1995 price list is the 1600 Classic. This kit reduces the car to its bare bones but is still comprehensive. Aero-screens instead of a full windscreen, no fuel gauge and just a speedo in the way of dashboard instruments. £8450 plus delivery is the cost of this and you shouldn't need to spend a single penny more to get the car completed. As it happens, most customers will take

a look at the Classic and will then pay the extra to get the vehicle up to Classic SE specification.

Very few bare bones Classics have been sold, which shows that UK buyers are prepared to shell out more for their Seven than the factory might have thought. Apart from the now-deceased JPE kits, sold at around £33,750, the most expensive standard road Caterham CKD kit is the Vauxhall-powered HPC at £18,200 inclusive of VAT.

In order to reassure the less optimistic mechanics of this world, Caterham supplies its kits with an enormous build manual and a video entitled *Building the Legend*. The manual itself is heavy on the text and light on drawings. There are no photos in its pages but the video compensates for this. The fact that so much is done by the factory means that there is precious little to get caught out by. No messing around with donor cars and no taking bits to the factory for modification or exchange. That really represents excellent value for money, if you can come up with the cash in one big lump.

For the driver who thinks that a GTI is quick or that an MR2 handles, even the most basic, live-axled Caterham must be a revelation on the road. Top speed is limited by aerodynamics and the general discomfort of driving with or without the hood in place. The key to the whole experience is in the handling and roadholding. "It's quite possible for a K-Series to beat a V8-powered opponent on the road or track," says Andrew Noble.

With superb suspension feel, masses of grip and traction, the Seven is a master of dry roads. In the wet, a tendency to oversteer is revealed, along with a superb throttle control of the back end. It might be a little daunting for the driver of today's understeering production car but it really is the essence of genuine sports car driving. Getting the tail out isn't drama, it's fun, and it needn't lead to an emergency situation every time. The High Performance Course recommended by Caterham will give the less confident a really good grounding in proper car driving.

Ford's X-flow, turned into something rather lusty by Caterham's own performance modifications, suits both the live axle and deDion cars really well. With the four-speed box, motorway trips are tiresome but country lane sprinting is exhilarating – all with the benefit of knowing that it can be done without tuning an engine to the point of hysteria.

If the chance is taken to drive a more expensive model, perhaps fitted with a twin-cam Vauxhall engine, it becomes apparent that the chassis and brakes are supremely confident. After only a few miles, "More Power!" is the cry. These are not like lumbering V8s which keep drivers in a perpetual state of fear lest the throttle be too heavily depressed, resulting in an instant spin. This is class and predictability.

Sevens are also much favoured for their unpretentious operating requirements. The driver doesn't have to be a muscled hulk to manage the steering wheel – unlike some of the more outrageous front drive hatches available. Sensitivity is far more important when driving this car and the rewards are remarkable. Thrashing around on a bright morning, in a remote country area, is the ultimate scenario. Because the controls fall to hand and foot so well, the driver's attention can be wholly focused on road position and steering. Everything else seems to happen automatically, in a seemingly magical fashion. They're that good.

Performance Car magazine said of the limited edition JPE: "This car is fast with a capital F...The F40 is going to get stuffed out of sight." That last comment referred to a 0-100-0mph test where the JPE averaged 13.1 seconds compared to the Ferrari F40's 15.9 seconds! Enough said.

The Future

It seems a little strange that Caterham Cars has stuck so rigidly to the Seven theme throughout its long association with the car. In the early days of their affiliation with Lotus, they had been obliged to take on an Elite demonstrator as well as the Seven but nothing really came of this. Hasn't there been a temptation to look into something new, a different model altogether? After all, mastery of the Super Seven's chassis and suspension designs must have given the company a thorough understanding of such principles. Something that they could use to design a competent new car.

In 1993 this proposition wasn't met with complete derision by director Andrew Noble. "We have looked at other projects but it's very difficult to plough your efforts into something new when you're still improving what you already have." At that time it wasn't possible to discover just what other projects had been looked at. However, we now know that the company did more than just look at

other projects, following its launched of the new Caterham 21 at the 1994 Birmingham Motor Show. This fully enclosed GRP bodied roadster mounted on a modified Seven chassis and running gear promises to take the company into new markets. Sold in near complete form, with prices beginning just under the £20,000 mark, Caterham will find itself up against the likes of the new MGF, Fiat Barchetta and, of course, TVR.

With the exception of the new 21, evidence of Caterham's single-minded crusade to refine the Seven forever and a day is shown in the distinct lack of odd concept cars to have come from the Caterham stable. Other than various Seven derivatives, the company's exhibits at the mainstream and kit car shows throughout the land have always been wholly Seven-orientated.

What about mid-engined formats? Many of today's production cars are based on front-drive componentry which can be a little expensive to convert to rear-drive for the Caterham. Isn't it tempting to put a complete front-drive engine and gearbox unit behind the occupants in some sort of new exotic?

"The mid-engined argument just doesn't bear scrutiny. The Seven has superb front to rear weight distribution – it's probably more mid-engined than most other cars on the market." There was a time when the factory set its cars up to understeer mildly, as the mainstream motoring press seemed to think that understeer was what everyone wanted. "After the rave reviews for the Mazda MX5, which oversteers, we have altered the Seven to oversteer mildly. There's nothing more enjoyable than driving a

Caterham 21 is the company's first all new car since it took on the Seven in 1973. Certainly looks worth the wait.

Sales development abroad was recently recognised when the company was awarded the Queen's Award For Export.

Caterham in the wet." Obviously no need for a mid-engined coupe there.

What about further developments for the Sevens themselves? As mentioned before, the cars are always changing. Is there an imminent demise of the live-axled cars on the cards? Stocks of the new Kent engines seem set to last for a few years and there may be a system for supplying reconditioned examples after that. More importantly, the Ital axle stocks won't last forever and the Classic kits are already being supplied with reconditioned axles and gearboxes, precluding them from current prefix registration marks.

The curious emissions regulations apparently give leave for companies to supply engines which need only comply with emissions regulations in force at the date of manufacture of that engine. Hence the older stocks of engines such as the X-flow and the first Vauxhall units don't necessarily require complex induction and exhaust componentry. Cosworth still supplies the BDR 1700, for instance, despite much talk of its final demise. They're obviously having difficulty getting new Ford blocks for that particular engine conversion.

Has Caterham looked into making its own engines at all? Obviously they have. "It's not really viable because of the high development and manufacturing costs. Even if we were just making cylinder head conversions, we'd probably have to sell around 2500 units a year to make it worthwhile. It would have to be a high-volume, high-cost exercise."

Either way, there are still plenty of good engines coming from the mainstream industry, all of which can be made to comply with worldwide regulations. "There may be an 1800cc replacement for the Vauxhall 2-litre HPC unit. We will have to make sure that we keep up to date on new developments like that." Engines from other manufacturers? No negative answer there, but no further information either.

Although there has been a trickle of Caterhams going into the very well protected USA, there hasn't yet been a full-scale assault on the turn-key car market there. "We are putting the Seven through all the relevant additional tests for the USA. Such alterations as putting the fuel tank within the car's wheelbase will have to be done but we don't foresee the need for full Type Approval yet. The key to selling abroad is to sell in Sterling. Otherwise, exchange rates fluctuate too much." That's a problem when unit profit margins are being kept to a minimum for competitive pricing, especially as far as the turn-key cars are concerned.

It's amazing to see that a company can still be as perceptive about potential development of their cars this far along the line. Work on the Seven range goes on and on and the car gets better and better, without reverting to some trendy modern bubble-shaped exterior for aerodynamic purposes. It's a question of making the car faster, with better handling, at the right price.

"We appreciate that we may be competing with the new kitchen, stereo or family hatchback, so there has to be some compromise between price and performance." Andrew Noble tells us that the JPE models didn't make a profit for Caterham, despite their £33,000+ price tag. "The engines alone cost us £12,000 without the overheads." Still, it got them into the *Guinness Book of Records,* didn't it? Even so, the fact that the vehicle has to be saleable at the end of the day doesn't stop the factory trying for ultimates. "We are here to produce the best car," asserts Mr. Noble. "We do it because we love it." There's plenty of evidence of that to be found when the factory is visited.

What about the future of the kit car scene in the UK? For a start, the availability of at least two turn-key Caterhams would cushion the blow if the government legislated heavily against amateur-built kits. "I hope the Super-MOT will happen," says Andrew. "We need better controls on amateur built cars in this country." That is indicative of the Caterham crusade for better quality in the market but there doesn't seem to be an underlying agenda for ditching kits in favour of completed cars. Thank goodness. It would be a shame to see the Seven available only as a really up-market investment. Prices for the completed K-Series and HPC cars are a shade under £15,000 and £20,000 respectively and the majority of UK buyers spend less than that.

· In order to stimulate demand and to take advantage of the healthy second-hand market for Caterhams, the company has introduced a very tempting buy-back scheme which encompasses amateur-built kits. The Caterham owner will be given a guaranteed price for a used Seven when putting in an order for a new kit. That means that a progression up the specification ladder is easier and covers the owner against any (very unlikely) down-turn in the value of the car.

Over the last 12 months, Caterham have yet again reorganised the Crayford production premises in Unit 2. Partition walls have been removed and replaced in order to streamline the assembly of kits and completed cars. This might well be linked to the increasing importance of fully built cars to the company. Systems are constantly being devised to smooth the transition from bare chassis to CKD, Component Form or turn-key car.

Having witnessed the scale and the expertise of the Caterham empire, the newcomer will have a good idea of what constitutes quality and progress in specialist car manufacture. In a way, it's the showpiece of the kit car world, telling us that there is a respectable future for kit manufacturers with the right attitude towards reinvestment and progress.

Others are beginning to emulate this evolution, with some excellent kit cars, but there's still a lot of competition for a limited number of buyers and the market is by no means completely out of recession. For the time being at least, British car enthusiasts are able to buy and build an incredible sporting car which is held in motoring awe by other countries which aren't so lucky. How many other motor manufacturers could boast that they are where they are through such severe specialisation? Mr. Noble sums it all up: "We want to be extreme..."

Looking good for the future. Caterham continues to go from strength to strength. Long may it continue.

Chapter 3

Tiger Super Six

A Brief History

Today's Tiger Super Six is a bold, aggressive, no-frills statement of sporting intent. With an exceptionally strong chassis, race-bred suspension and a carefully sculptured functional prettiness, this particular strain of the sevenesque breed looks mean and means business. No surprise, then, that in terms of performance, handling and on-the-limit roadholding, the car brims with confidence.

The story of its background, however, could hardly be more different: a long, restless saga of trouble and uncertainty with the Super Six's predecessor, the South African made RM Seven – not a car that made Caterham and Westfield's management people at all happy. At the end of the day, there weren't that many smiles on the face of Tiger boss Jim Dudley, either!

Jim Dudley, Tiger Cars' main man, with the company's Tiger Super Six SSI.

As a young lad living in London's Bexley Heath area, Jim was mad keen on cycling and would often thrash down to Dartford for both the exercise and the thrill of speed. It was here that he regularly passed a kart and motorsport centre managed by Tony Brise, the man who later became a notable racing driver and very close friend of Graham Hill (and who, tragically, died with Hill when their light aircraft crashed). Karting didn't do anything much for the young Dudley, but the sight one day of a full size, grown-up Lotus version sitting outside the centre really fired up his imagination. Indeed, the encounter was to have a more significant effect on the man's life than he could ever have guessed.

A qualified garage mechanic since 1969, Jim found himself just aching to get his hands on a Lotus Seven and enjoy the driving exhilaration it offered. The dream was realised when he bought an early '60s 1600cc powered Series One example from a Scottish enthusiast. £450 was the price agreed, including all expenses incurred by the vendor, who'd driven the raw little roadster some 450 miles from Scotland in hope!

From that day on, Jim began an amazing love affair with Sevens of various types. "I bought a different example of either a Lotus or a Caterham every year until early 1989," he recalls, "and not long after that I set up Tiger Cars to make something very similar. In all, I must have owned well over 50 Sevens in my time, building at least ten of them from kits. I've just been mad about them for as long as I can remember."

Behind the affair was a pleasurable mix of hobby and business themes. Early on, several of the Lotuses were used for competition – sprints, hillclimbs etc. Later, after Caterham Cars had acquired the

The South African based RM Seven was Jim's first foray into kit car manufacturing but its similarity with both the Caterham's styling and Westfield's suspension set-up caused no end of trouble.

manufacturing rights, Jim built several cars for other people. Whatever the period, most of the cars were uprated and tuned to provide ultimate performance. Any form of repair, however serious, was like second nature to a pure enthusiast who knew Sevens like the back of his hand.

By the 1980s, Jim was running a successful VW parts company, Volkshouse, from premises in the old tram stabling sheds at Plumstead, East London, as well as a large modern premises in Deptford. Though profitable, the business wasn't personally fulfilling: in truth, the boss was just itching to get into manufacturing specialist cars. A new interpretation of the classic Seven theme would fit the bill nicely...

Drawings were done and a start was made on fabricating the first chassis. The car's name was to be Tiger Six. But full and proper development of such a project takes time and when a chance look at a South African car magazine had Jim captured by a Caterham lookalike, the RM Seven, he couldn't resist some further investigation. Following extensive telephone negotiations with the manufacturer, the first RM to reach UK soil arrived early in 1990, just in time to debut at the annual Sports and Kit Car Show at Stafford in March.

Well finished and nicely detailed, the car attracted plenty of praise, even at a projected price of around

£11,000 in almost complete form. The multi-tubular chassis looked strong and carried double-wishbone front suspension and a live axle at the rear. Power was by Ford CVH 1600 with the Kent engine as an alternative. "A serious contender amongst similar looking performance roadsters," said *Which Kit?* magazine in an issue carrying the resplendent looking dark green chariot on its cover.

Trouble was, the RM Seven's styling did look a little too close to the Caterham's for comfort – for Jim Dudley's comfort. He was rather disturbed about the chassis design, too: it looked uncannily close to Westfield's SE frame. Only on the strict promise of legal help, if necessary, from the South African factory were another five complete kits ordered by Tiger Cars – at a cost of around £35,000. It was to be money down the drain...

First sign of big trouble for Tiger Cars was a High Court writ from Westfield Sportscars concerning chassis design copyright. Next, after one of the imported kits had been assembled and displayed at the big 1990 Stoneleigh kit car extravaganza, a writ from Caterham Cars arrived alleging passing-off over body styling. Serious legal problems, indeed, but what never did materialise was the legal help from Port Elizabeth, South Africa, home of RM.

"Without the back-up promised by RM," recalls Jim Dudley ruefully, "I felt it wasn't worth fighting. I was so pissed-off with all the legal stuff going on and writs flying around that I soon agreed to hand over to Caterham Cars six RM Sevens in varying stages of completion, all less engines and gearboxes. I also paid the legal costs for both Caterham and Westfield. In fact, by that time I was very glad to see the back of it all. Needless to say, I was slightly upset about losing over £40,000!"

Amazingly, one thing the whole sorry saga didn't

Below: Fitted with a CVH engine, the RM Seven was bang up to date with engine choice. Bottom: RM Seven didn't last long but the exotic 250 LM sports coupe is currently under redevelopment.

do was ruin the man's enthusiasm for minimalist sporting chariots of pure performance intentions. He smiles at the memory: "By the time Caterham picked up the RM cars, I'd done all the final chassis, suspension and body development on the prototype Tiger Six. I'll never forget what the Caterham representative said when I showed him the Six: 'You'd better let us inspect that fully before you put it on the road.' I interpreted it as a bit of a threat, and it really got my determination going."

Sure enough, Jim was in no mood to waste any more time. Painted a medium shade of blue and powered by a 1600 CVH, the prototype Tiger Six made its debut at Sandown Park, Esher, in August 1990. With front cycle wings, a wide nose, plenty of bulges and a high-ish bonnet line, it looked aggressive in the fashion made famous by the Lotus Six and early examples of the Seven breed. The car looked like it meant business alright, a feature that wasn't lost on the kit car buying public. Interest was strong and the Tiger's future looked to have potential.

One aspect Jim was particularly keen on for his new baby was an especially strong spaceframe chassis. "I'd really hammered all my Lotus Sevens on both road and track, and if I could have improved on one thing, it would have been overall strength. The cars needed greater side impact protection, too. I wasn't worried about any slight weight penalty that might be incurred in achieving great strength and safety in the Six."

By mid-1991 the nicely engineered Six was in regular production and Jim Dudley's dream had finally materialised. Some 25-30 body/chassis units were made in the first 12 months' production in the sprawling old Tramyard buildings in southeast London, a decent figure considering the deep recession that was just beginning to affect all consumer markets.

For their £1695 + VAT, customers received the full multi-tubular spaceframe chassis (made from 1.5" square section 16-gauge tube), all GRP and aluminium bodywork and interior panels. The extras list was comprehensive, and in 1991 it was claimed that around £5000 expenditure was plenty enough to see a good example roadworthy.

What the builder had to supply was the assembly skill, the powertrain and the running gear. Front suspension was a combination of modified VW Golf uprights and lower wishbones with laser cut steel upper wishbones and ventilated Golf discs, while at the rear was a Ford Cortina live axle located by fabricated tubular steel trailing arms. Steering came courtesy of a blend of Escort rack and Golf column. An optional power unit was the Ford Kent engine, with the Pinto 2-litre joining the list upon the introduction of the evolution Super Six model.

Distinguishing this car visually were the new nose moulding and revised GRP bonnet with large power bulge. Initially, the latter had been necessary to accommodate the Pinto's extra height but the bulge was felt by Jim Dudley to suit particularly well the car's aggressive image and so was made standard. Likewise the name Super Six.

1994 saw the securing of a large order for fully built cars to Japan and Tiger took this opportunity to continue developing the Super Six, with improved fibreglass mouldings and minor suspension revisions. The company's most recent development has been a move out of the ramshackle Tramyard works and into new improved premises close by in Charlton.

Tiger Today

As has always been Tiger's policy, nearly everything needed to produce a Tiger kit is manufactured in-house. It's the normal state of affairs for many specialist car manufacturers. Sub-contracting important kit components such as bodies and chassis can be beneficial as the buyer can simply return any sub- standard goods for replacement. However, the ups and downs of demand can also create problems in the smooth supply of goods at short notice. If it's all done by your own staff, then at

Above and top: The first wholly Tiger designed car was the Tiger Six seen here when first revealed at the Sandown Kit Car Show in 1990. Below: It was based on a substantial spaceframe chassis.

least you'll have control over schedules and small production niggles.

Tiger's recently acquired new unit is in sharp contrast to the old Tramyard works. Based in one large 10,000 sq.ft. unit one is immediately presented with the huge assembly area where any number of kits can be seen in varying stages of assembly. Many of the part assembled cars will be destined for the new Japanese deal secured by the company in 1994, but body/chassis kits for UK customers are also in evidence, awaiting collection.

During our visit, an Super Six chassis was being fitted with its galvanised steel floor sheets, which are hand-riveted in place as an optional extra. Many customers opt for the CBFC kit (chassis/body fitted, with colour) which provides most inner and

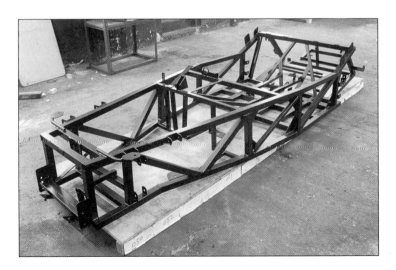

The fitment of tall 2-litre Pinto engines (below) led to the development of a fibreglass bonnet with power bulge that added to the car's already aggressive stance. Interior was well up to standard (right).

outer body fitment and a paint finish.

At the time of our visit, spray work was still being undertaken at the old Tramyard works while the purpose built spray booth is completed at the new factory. It was occupied by yet another Super Six car, receiving the final touches to its Glasurit spray finish. Jim's son Paul appears to be the paintwork expert. With 4000 colour options on offer, he's getting a bit busy these days.

Back at the new factory a large room on the ground floor has been dedicated to the fabrication department. This area is dominated by the main jigs for the Super Six and SSI (independent rear suspension) chassis. Other tools are crammed into this area – equipment for cutting steel tubes plus various types of welding systems, including gas and MIG.

Also on the ground floor you'll find an ever developing parts department required to cater for the fully built cars for Japan and an increasing number of UK kits which are ordered in comprehensive form. Tiger was one of the first of it type to offer a comprehensive package, with everything needed to complete a basic car, at a highly competitive price. The company has not yet tried for Low Volume Type Approval in the UK, which would allow it to sell fully built cars here, but the comprehensive kit package is proving very popular.

Next to the stores is a quite pleasant little waiting room, where prospective customers can read Tiger's literature while they await a test drive in one of the company's demonstrators, or perhaps a tour of the new factory. On from here is a small office where the increasing amount of paperwork required for fully built cars and comprehensive kits is organised into some form of order.

Upstairs at the new unit one finds the laminating room where all the various fibreglass panels are made. Tiger has continually developed its GRP work and current kits are turned out to a highly impressive standard. Also upstairs one finds the trimming department, where comprehensive carpet sets and seats are assembled into packages for the various kits about to leave the works. Jim Dudley had only recently moved into the new factory on our most recent visit and certain areas were still yet to be finally sorted out. Despite this, the new unit is a major step forward for Tiger and, apart from easing production, it should also install into customers a greater confidence in the company's operation compared to the old workshops.

At the moment, one part-time and ten full-time staff members are to be found at Tiger Cars. All of the chassis welders have been approved by the Specialist Transport Advisory and Testing Utility Society to British Standards conformity (Tiger Cars is a member of STATUS and of the RMIF). The jigs look solid and well designed – plenty of labour time goes into cutting, bending and shaping the 1.5" square section tubes from which the chassis are predominantly made. Jim's fabrication shop also takes care of the modifications which are made to the various VW and Ford donor parts. Most of the unique suspension components are manufactured in-house. Whereas the price list offers a choice of engines, of which the most popular fitment is currently the 2-litre Pinto OHC four, Tiger don't actually do the engine reconditioning or re-manufacturing. It's more likely that a complete engine and gearbox will be ordered in or that a standard or performance engine will be assembled by their staff, after the machining has been done by external experts. The Japanese cars all go out with Vulcan Engines prepared 1700cc Ford X-flows or Dunnell Engines prepared 2-litre Zetec units. Both can be

The Tiger's curvaceous styling has set it apart from the ultra simple styling of some of its competitors and, as such, found a healthy following.

ordered by the UK customer.

Laser cutting has been adopted as the best method for shaping the steel upper wishbones of the Super Six and the SSI and several other steel components are also produced in this way. Again, that's a job that you have to farm out. Lasers are still pretty expensive on the whole!

The SSI structure comes automatically with powder coating and obviously this is also a process which is best left to experts with the right equipment. The lower perimeter tubes have plastic end caps, which permit Waxoyling or other rust-inhibiting processes.

Jim Dudley is usually to be found overseeing an aspect of the production process or giving guidance as to scheduling. Not for him the suit and tie in an air-conditioned environment. It's still very much a hands-on approach from the management. In effect, the Tigers are still pretty new to the market and the staff is still en route to finalising the smooth and automatic production procedures which you will see in operation at the biggest companies.

Up to now, though, Jim has been continually developing the Super Six. The independent SSI is also currently being refettled. It's important to have a strong involvement in the production processes when you're the one instituting new designs and systems. This is the sort of flexibility which allows small specialist car producers to jump forward in leaps and bounds, where the hamstrung production car manufacturers must expensively type approve any

Engine installations have been varied. This Fiat 1600cc twin-cam engine (top) certainly looks the part whilst the 1600cc Ford X- flow powered example (above) is especially neat. Both are customer built cars. Below: Interior trim can be made very tidy.

significant new parts and designs, let alone processes.

The customer is not politely guided away from the heart of the matter at Tiger Cars, and all the production work can be seen at first hand. Jim's approach to design and to customer relations are already making the Tiger popular with both new and experienced kit builders and it looks like it may well end up with an SSI (or similar) Tiger Six going for Limited Volume Type Approval when the economy picks up. That's a good indication of serious intent for the future.

Current Models

Tiger Cars has now settled on two model types for the time being. Their popular live-axled Super Six and the independent rear suspension model, the SSI. The latter was first driven by the kit car press in July 1993. Production of these two subtly different cars seems to be set for a prolonged run, especially as they have both been very well received.

Because of the lower budget required for completion of a home build, the Super Six will

Above: Which Kit? magazine built its own Tiger Super Six in 1993. Powered by a 2.1-litre Ford Pinto engine it was viciously quick with handling to match.

probably remain the more popular option with amateur car builders around the country. There's still no shortage of the defunct Cortina donor and the relevant servicing components for these vehicles.

There are still two very polarised schools of thought vis a vis rear suspension options. Those who think that the live axle is outmoded and an encumbrance due to heavy unsprung weight and those who think that a good live axle set-up is as much as you need.

Fortunately, there are enough believers in each alternative to justify successful production of both options. Needless to say, chassis and body variations

Below: Line of sight instruments can work but it's a tight fit. Golf column stalk controls are excellent. Bottom: Golf lower front wishbone clearly visible here. Works well, too.

exist between these models and the SSI shows many alterations which you could interpret as potential Limited Volume Type Approval concessions.

Tiger's unique nose aperture shape and integral 'composite' bonnet bulges are still to be found in the more recent SSI model but the mouldings are nearly all dimensionally different from those of the Super Six. Jim has put an awful lot of work into refining the shape of the panels to cover external protrusions and to generally smooth out the contours of the car. That's the kind of thing that LVTA requires.

Because the SSI's chassis is also completely different to that of the Super Six, the engine choice will be marginally greater. Jim has already squeezed a Rover V8 into the standard Super Six chassis but the SSI will probably accommodate it much more easily – bonnet bulges are slightly different and the side panels are alloy, not GRP.

Fundamentally, both the Super Six and the SSI are based around chassis of similar design. The earlier Super Six chassis features a very well cross-braced floor section with most of its beam and torsional rigidity coming from triangulated perimeter, backbone and bulkhead sections. Very little extra stiffness is derived from the sheet steel, alloy and GRP panelling.

Tiger Cars removes the old suspension mounting points from the Cortina Mk.4 or 5 live axle, supplied usually by the customer, and welds into place a selection of new pick-ups. These will accommodate a pair of offset radius rods each side of the axle, a Panhard rod and twin Spax or AVO adjustable coil-over shock absorbers. The radius rods feature metalastic bushes and the springs are rated at between 150 and 180 pounds for the rear.

Basically, the axle is inserted into the rear framework of the chassis from one side and supported while the locating components are positioned. Rear brakes are the standard Cortina drums but the handbrake mechanism is cleverly modified for the Tiger.

It's a neat and compact way of mounting a live axle, and the lateral location offered by a long Panhard rod means that the tunnel width can be kept to a minimum. The builder must ensure that any panelling work done, especially in the rear bulkhead area, leaves room for the vertical travel of the axle, differential nose and flange.

Up at the front, Jim has designed a unique suspension assembly which has worked very efficiently for the Super Six. This includes a new laser-cut top wishbone each side and a selection of other components from the VW Golf donor. Some of these must be modified by Tiger prior to fitment.

Another pair of Spax or AVO coil-overs, identical to those at the rear, fits between the chassis upper rail and the Golf lower wishbone (special Tiger lower wishbones have been developed to replace the Golf

Above: Tiger continually develops the Super Six. This example features a new interior (left) while engine bay has new pedal box moulding and heater housing (below). Vulcan prepared engine is a beauty.

bonnet bulge is that the ubiquitous Pinto donor engine is pretty tall, even if fitted with after-market side-draught carburettors and a more compact sump. Never mind, the engine bay still offers plenty of room in terms of length and servicing access and there's a specially made radiator to fit behind the nosecone.

Don't underestimate the size of the Super Six,

item should the customer prefer). Spring rates between 200 and 225 pounds are used here, depending upon engine weight. Front brakes are Golf GTI calipers and discs, with a Beetle type dual circuit master cylinder and no servo. A special brake pipe kit is supplied by Tiger for all of their models.

Even the upright/stub axle is Golf and the rear axle is modified to offer a Golf wheel stud PCD pattern, meaning that all of the specially made alloy wheels are a Golf fit for the Super Six. The offset has been chosen specifically for the Tiger, though. Curiously, Jim chose the Escort Mk.2 steering rack for the Super Six and builders must shorten the track rods a little prior to fitment. This gives a noticeably narrower track at the front than at the rear.

Part of the reason for that generous

though. It may seem much the same as others in its general class but it's actually quite a large car. There's a gear lever extension mechanism fitted with the purpose of bringing the lever back within comfortable reach of the driver and, using the simple flat seat cushion option, a driver of over six feet tall can be accommodated nicely. Last, but not least, in the list of commendations is the Super Six's excellent build manual. Some 200 pages of precise instructions with illustrations. We await a similar publication for the SSI.

When the SSI is placed alongside the Super Six, you can start to see just how many differences there are. It's a bigger car all round. All of the panels are different in one way or another and there's a lot more subtle detail work. Under the skin, you'll see that the chassis is also completely different, as are many of the suspension components.

Like most manufacturers who have chosen to offer an independent rear suspension option, Tiger have gone for a system based on the standard Ford Sierra parts. (Consult them before using components from the XR4x4, XR4i and Cosworth). The various 1.6, 1.8, 2-litre, 2.3-litre and even diesel models are suitable for the rear suspension, which is used full width and is about the same track as the Cortina.

Builders will find that many Sierras will be good donor vehicles if you choose one with the engine and gearbox that you prefer. Out goes the huge, curved tube rear subframe from the Sierra, leaving the basic differential unit, half-shafts and hubs/drum brakes. Discs are an optional rear fitment but most Sierra donors won't have these.

Here you can see the difference between the Tiger's standard front suspension (left) and that fitted to the new independent rear suspension car (right).

In order to properly locate the rear suspension, Jim has designed the obvious chassis mounts for the differential, which is very solidly located, and a completely new rear suspension assembly. The latter originally involved a pair of carefully fabricated, tapered box section trailing arms, one each side of the car. Into the trailing end of each arm went the Sierra hub/stub axle/drum brake mechanisms. Further location of the Tiger trailing arms was offered by a pair of tubular track control arms each side, one above and one below the rear end of each trailing arm. The rods were rubber bushed and their mounts were detachable from the chassis to allow for camber adjustment via shims.

This original set-up received very good reviews when tested in the first SSI demonstrator but Tiger's Jim Dudley is currently redeveloping the system into a more conventional double wishbone arrangement. The reasons for this are twofold. The first is that it allows for a prettier looking suspension which is particularly important for Tiger's foreign markets. The second is that a forthcoming Tiger is about to receive an engine delivering over 300bhp and it was felt that the original set-up would struggle to deal with such large amounts of power.

As ever, the Spax or AVO coil-overs are the same front and rear on the SSI, with different spring rates depending upon the engine weight, horsepower and intended use of the car. Major changes are to be found at the front of the SSI when compared to the standard Super Six. Here we see a much more standard set-up relying on a combination of special and Cortina parts. Out with the VW contingent. The SSI looks much wider than the Super Six mainly because it's wider at the front. There's now a Cortina steering rack instead of an Escort Mk.2 item. Builders are also helped by the fact that the forged front uprights, the calipers and discs are all Cortina Mk.4 or 5, meaning that the wheel stud PCD fitment is the same front and rear.

Completely new components have been designed for the highly adjustable front suspension of the SSI. Those Cortina uprights are located by tubular upper and lower track control arms which, in turn, are triangulated with semi-trailing tie rods of adjustable length. This effectively means upper and lower tubular

Above: The Tiger SSI is the company's independent rear suspension model. This example in powered by a 1.8-litre Ford Zetec engine fitted with a catalytic converter (left).

wishbones adjustable for castor etc. Because of the high Cortina content up front, cost has been controlled – although it's obviously still not a one-donor car.

Some themes remain the same. No anti roll bars, a modified Tiger handbrake mechanism, gear lever extension assembly and a purpose made brake line kit. The original SSI demonstrator was fitted with a new Ford Zeta 1.8 twin-cam motor and catalytic converter.

This last point has obviously been the result of a large volume of development work and assembly time. You will know that modern emission control engines come with all manner of tubes, ducts, sensors, mouldings and carapaces which are inevitably designed for the wrong type of under-bonnet area.

Even so, Tiger have fitted their example nicely and have already commissioned a suitable off-the-shelf

Above: Rover V8 engines have been fitted to the Tiger. You can just see the carburettor tops poking out of the bonnet of this first prototype. Below: Club meetings at Goodwood race circuit are extremely popular.

wiring loom (available for all their engine options). The only slight eye-sore is the small converter itself which is, er, modified and crammed in just ahead of the offside footwell.

Tiger seem to stick with side-exit exhausts only but on the first demonstrator the catalytic converter had been carefully tucked away inside the engine bay. It's a very tight squeeze and since then the company has had a special catalytic converter made up that will sit on the outside of the car, under a heat shield just in front of the main exhaust box.

Having taken the plunge to create a new chassis, Jim has also, sensibly, incorporated extra width for the SSI's occupants. This has meant that normal or smaller-sized customers can opt for more luxurious seats and that larger folk can benefit from every inch of extra space by using basic seat squabs.

Closer inspection reveals the different nosecone contours, hiding much of the front suspension inboard mounting points, a new dash/scuttle moulding with its integral screen base moulding and even rear light pedestals moulded into the rear wings. They are just a few of the less visible revisions.

In early 1995, the basic live-axled Super Six kit, with powder coated and pre-panelled chassis and 2-pack painted body (dropped in place on the chassis) would have cost you £2,200 + VAT. The basic SSI kit, which comes with a powder coated chassis, much of the bodywork pre-fitted and all paintwork complete, will weigh in at around £2,500 once the new rear suspension set-up has been finalised. Both packages are extremely good value for money but each prospective customer must obviously budget for extra components from Tiger's price lists. We found that the various stages of partial builds offered ex-factory were also extremely good value.

It's a sensible two-kit line up but when you take

into account engine options from 1100cc Kent X-flow up to the Rover V8, there's plenty of variation to be had along the way. Will the SSI be the next sevenesque car to get Limited Volume Type Approval? A distinct possibility. We can't get Jim to comment further on the prospect...

Tiger on the road

Previous visits have shown us that the live-axled Super Six had already become a street-wise predator. Extreme traction and grip with firm suspension feel and a good deal of steering feedback.

It must be said that the cars of this ilk, fitted with the Cortina axle, do feel rather wide. The rear wings tend to protrude generously from the relatively

Above: Track testing the V8 Tiger at Goodwood. On the track you can just make out a McLaren F1! Below: Which Kit?'s own car being put through its paces on the famous circuit.

Q209 RGH

The recent move to larger premises should greatly ease production. Many of these cars are heading for foreign shores.

narrow main body and you can be fooled for a moment into forgetting just how wide the cars really are! Think twice before trying to squeeze through that gap!

Super Six demo cars showed Jim's suspension set-ups to be functional and free from such annoying traits as bump steer and rear axle steer. Admittedly, the Cortina live axle isn't a lightweight thing and the more demanding driver could still detect that the high-ish unsprung weight was adding some bumpiness and loss of grip on choppy or otherwise rough corners.

There was just sufficient cockpit width and length for this six- foot driver of broad frame but it was a touch too restricted on footwell width at the pedal end. Size ten feet in old trainers were a bit of a squeeze, calling for some degree of care when operating the pedals energetically. Golf Mk.1 column stalks make the car very user-friendly around town and the simple weather gear and tonneau are easy to fit, even if the hood isn't a fold-down system.

Driving the original independent SSI puts the icing on the cake as far as handling is concerned. This is to be expected from an IRS evolution model. It feels even wider, due to the Cortina front track, and again demonstrates that Jim has been able to design a bump steer-free, tramp-free, rear steer-free suspension system right from the word go.

Absolutely masses of traction and grip in the dry and very commendable in the wet. As with the Super Six, there's a hint of initial understeer but you can

drive the thing so hard into and around corners that when the back end starts to complain, the throttle is an excellent governor of the eventual oversteer. If you get the SSI sideways in the dry, though, you're trying very hard indeed.

Perhaps the best aspect of the SSI is its success in doing what the live-axled Super Six can't. That means that it can put the power down and retain grip while cornering on dodgy and very broken surfaces. The net effect of the lower unsprung weight is a great improvement in rear suspension smoothness and certainty. It's actually not so important for the track racer, who often benefits from the best surfaces but it does make a difference to the country-laner, driving in all conditions.

It must be said that the expensive-but-cleaner Zeta engine pulls really well from relatively low RPM. It doesn't benefit from red-line revs and you don't often need to take it there for some very high-speed thrills. Both Tiger chassis eagerly demand more BHP than most four-cylinder motors seem prepared to deliver!

As a matter of interest, the usually raucous exhaust note of the Tiger side-pipe system is very effectively muted by the addition of the catalytic converter. It's still a respectable buzz but it lacks the top end crackle. You could drive this car all day without a thumping headache at the end of it! Very civilised indeed.

Criticisms? The extra cockpit width is welcome but there's still the same lack of space at the footwell end for this driver. Both of the demonstrators have dashboard configurations which seem intent on hiding the speedo and tacho while revealing the temperature and oil pressure gauges to best effect. Happily, it's the kit builder who decides where the clocks go. GRP seemed generally good but early star crazes had appeared on the front cycle wings and on the bonnet.

Praise must be aimed at the general levels of user-friendliness. The rear view and side mirrors were all perfectly functional — all too often they seem to be positioned more as decorations than anything else on small sports cars. Use of the Golf Mk.1 steering column plus stalks persists, to good effect.

Full harness belts, although very inconvenient to adjust and fit each time you take up residence in the Super Six or SSI, do offer good driver location. Very useful when you're pulling quite high lateral G-force.

Commendable performance for both cars in the rattle and squeak- proofing department, as well as in trim, carpet and dash finishing equipment. That's important for the kit builder who wants something a little more than just a bare bones road rocket.

We must say that the Tigers are serious performance cars, as well as being good kit build prospects for the amateur. Which Kit? magazine put together an extremely fast Pinto-powered Super Six in around four weeks. We will have to wait and see if the SSI conforms to this easy assembly tradition – it's still relatively new to the market but much of the early panelling is done prior to delivery.

Various appearances on the race track have shown the car in a good light but their relative rarity means that they have some way to go before notching up track victories in the quantities to which Caterham, Westfield and Sylva are accustomed. However, there are many Tigers still under construction and early buyers are now starting to produce some very mean cars. Keep your eye on this one.

The Future

As you might have gathered, Tiger Cars is not a company to stand still for long and it's a virtual full-time occupation keeping up with new developments at the factory. Typical of Tiger's manic development of its product is the introduction of a Super Six fitted

Tiger's Jim Dudley has seen the company develop despite beginning production just as the recession took hold of the UK economy. Below: Latest cars are particularly impressive.

with an automatic gearbox. Not a choice one might expect to find in such a car but one which, we are told, is surprisingly effective.

Accepting that the Tiger will be continually updated, what else can we expect from the company? Low Volume Type Approval appears a distinct possibility based on the new independent rear suspensioned car using a Ford 2-litre Zetec engine. It's an expensive business and Tiger is currently weighing up the pros and cons of pursuing such a goal.

With the increasing trend for manufacturers of this type of vehicle to rebody their cars in a more enclosing design, could Tiger be looking for a new design to fit onto the Tiger chassis? Codenamed the Tiger Meteor, the company is currently developing exactly such a machine for launch in early 1996. It'll be available as a kit and highly competitively priced.

Despite entering the kit car market at the very beginning of one of the worst recessions most of us can remember, Tiger Cars has doggedly established itself in this highly competitive market. Such is the company's drive, that few would bet against its continued success in the future.

Above: Specially fabricated lower wishbones can now be ordered to replace the standard Golf items. Below: Dunnell Engines prepared Zetec engine is a real screamer.

Despite continual development, the Tiger Super Six remains competitively priced within the sevenesque midfield.

Chapter 4

Sylva Striker

A Brief History

Jeremy Phillips' Sylva Autokits must rate as one of the longest established kit car concerns in the UK.

Jeremy Phillips outside the small Lincolnshire factory with the workforce behind him that produces the pretty little Striker and Stylus. An earlier Sylva Fury can be seen in the background.

Although Jeremy has kept his business small and has specialised in favour of the budget racing enthusiast, his success has nevertheless been consistent for years.

In the beginning, as it were, Jeremy was inspired by an older brother who was particularly into specialist British sports cars. Bentleys and even a Lotus 11 would appear at the Phillips' home in Southampton. His dad used to work as a Sergeant mechanic in the RAF, so there was a pretty strong technical and mechanical sympathy in the family.

This was to be the downfall of his sister's Morris 8, which, having been neglected for a short while, fell prey to Jeremy's early mechanical experimentations. Worried about various side effects of the hobby, Mrs. Phillips would regularly come downstairs at 11pm and disconnect the supply to the garage lighting so that Jeremy would get enough sleep for school. "There I was underneath a chassis and the lights would just go out." Unfortunately, the extension lead to the garage came from the house.

This was during his school career. Somehow, Jeremy ended up going to do an apprenticeship in design drawing between the ages of sixteen and twenty-one. This led to a sensible civil engineering post in an estimating department until he was twenty-four. Not a bad career choice as it turned out. The commercial buildings on which he worked very often featured metal frame construction and there was a lot to be learned about triangulation, stiffness and safety factors, let alone the properties of materials.

A two year stint working in the same field, but based in Canada, augmented his valuable experience in designing the complex 'joins' where several steel members would come together. "We would take on these fiddly and complex design jobs that no-one else wanted. I actually enjoyed the work and thought it

was quite a challenge." During this time, an unending stream of small sports cars would grace Jeremy's garage and drive. Most of them seemed to be Italian.

With a decade of design draughtsmanship experience, at the ripe old age of 26 Jeremy returned to these shores in 1976. At that time, the design business looked healthy, so he went into partnership with his brother. Soon after that, he bought and constructed an Arkley SS, a kind of traditional roadster body styling kit for an MG Midget. This was one of the few kits commonly available in those days.

Somehow, it led to a meeting between himself and another chap who was building high quality Arkley conversions for John Britten, a Morgan agent. This chap was Nick Green, who went on to produce the NG TA and then a whole range of rather successful MG based roadster kits under the NG banner. Nick voiced approval of Jeremy's own Arkley and they entered into negotiations with Mr.

Above: A youthful Jeremy Phillips in one of the very first Sylva Stars to be produced. Below: His next model, the Sylva Leader, was essentially a smoother styled Star with a redeveloped chassis.

Britten about designing and creating a completely new kit based on MG parts. Jeremy went ahead and penned a complex chassis for the live-axled car but nothing came of the joint venture in the end. Nick eventually went his own way, using a cruciform chassis for the TA, and Jeremy stayed with the spaceframe principle and did early design work for his first kit, the Star.

It was not until 1981 that the prototype Star chassis saw the light of day. It used a Vauxhall Viva 1256cc engine, Viva front subframe and suspension (similar to the Cortina's) and a Viva rear live axle. Jeremy used his own garage at home at Lymington, Hampshire, to build this chassis, design the bodywork

Below: The Leader, like every Sylva built to date, was no mean performer out on the track. Bottom: The very first Mk.1 Sylva Striker parked in front of several Leaders at the company's Hampshire base. Note how similar the rear wind is to that of the Leader.

and shape up the full size body plug. But by the time the final detailing was taking place, the whole project had been transferred northwards to his father's garage in Tathwell, Lincolnshire.

Another move took place before Sylva Star number two was built. Early in 1982 what was known as Sylva Autokits moved operations to a small factory in Mablethorpe, Lincs., at which base the Sylva Star moved into limited production. However, the need to make more money and pressures of work on the draughtsmanship side (such skills had been maintained part-time) contrived to force a further move in 1983, this time back to Hampshire. A small, modern factory was rented at Milford-on-Sea to continue Star production but Jeremy already had another set of design ideas to try out.

In 1985 the Sylva Leader appeared as an evolutionary version of the Star. It got a new chassis and body but continued the two-seater, performance-orientated line started by the Star. Each development of the chassis was leading to lighter and stiffer structures and plenty of mould-making was done to refine body shapes. Somewhere in the background, there was the idea for a Lotus Seven-inspired vehicle. Something which would look fairly different but have the same roots...

"Although the Leader was quite popular, I came to the conclusion that it was really a bit of a blind alley. I wanted to do something like the Seven but it had to be different, not just a copy." The Star and Leader projects were sold to Niall Johanson's Swindon Sportscars for royalty payments.

By that time, the first Striker chassis had already been assembled, so things were starting to hot up a bit. Jeremy wasn't making a mint in kit cars yet, though. The design business was really still subsidising the kit production and development. A handy source of financial as well as technical back-up.

The Striker was born very much as a trial project in between making Leaders. Built later in 1985, the prototype car used a standard Leader chassis with Viva front suspension and an Escort rear axle. For propulsion it received something quite new to the Sylva marque, a 1000cc Mazda RX3 rotary engine. Its body was very different, too – a basic affair, mostly in aluminium but with a rear end that

remained for a long time in 'plug' form. It was built, like most plugs, from foam, chipboard and body filler, all covered with Furane resin for a strong, hard finish, and the reason it didn't progress beyond that stage was because there never seemed to be any time to take a mould from it!

Only one Mk.1 Striker was ever produced and it was first owned by Jeremy's brother Mark (not a Captain in the army). Raced regularly, it sported the legend 'Rotary Rocket' and only received a proper glassfibre rear body section when Mark made a mould from the plug in an attempt to lighten the car and improve performance. "That car is still doing the rounds today," reflects Jeremy. "I might consider buying it back if I can track it down."

Early in 1986 emerged the Striker Mk.2, the car that was to truly establish the name. Restyled with an all-new Seven-inspired, but very distinctive, body, the Mk.2 represented a great leap forward from the Mk.1 and was generally considered very pretty.

Its chassis was a combination multi-tubular spaceframe with structural alloy sheets in and around the cockpit and bulkhead area. The most obvious departure from the norm was the use of rocker arm top front wishbones, activating inboard coil-over shock absorbers. Customers mostly required the Ford X-flow Kent engines and these were mounted as far back as possible for ideal weight distribution. The latter entailed shifting the engine over to the nearside a little, to retain sufficient footwell room for the pedals.

Above: Jeremy Phillips competing in an Mk.2 Striker with alloy rear bodywork. Below: Early Mazda powered Mk.1 behind an all GRP bodied Mk.2. The aerodynamic rear bodywork was later dropped. Opposite: The closest any Striker has come to the traditional sevenesque look. However, swept front wings have never been a popular option.

The prototype Mk.2 Striker was naturally out on the track as soon as possible. Powered by a 1600cc Ford cross-flow engine, it was initially raced by Stewart Beddow, who in 1985 had won the kit car racing championships in a Westfield Eleven. Stewart had a great time with the little car before handing it back to Jeremy for 1987's campaign. Co-driven by Jeremy and Chris Alford, and now powered by a Mazda RX7 rotary engine, the car saw plenty of success. It was this success that was of such great value in helping create regular demand for production Striker Mk.2s. Soon the Milford-on-Sea factory was buzzing with activity.

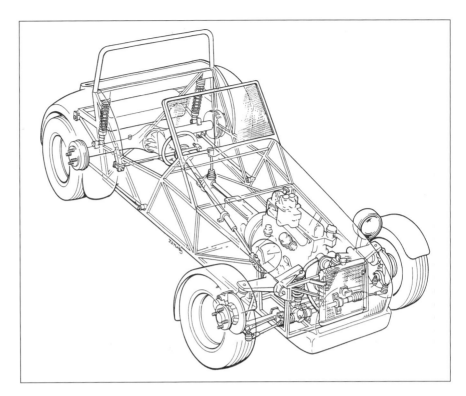

Before the Phillips roadshow again moved back up to Lincolnshire, early in 1988, a certain Mr. Paul Kuzan got very involved with the racing effort. He owned a Sylva Leader and spent a lot of time voluntarily helping out at the factory, when he wasn't at work in his high-powered computing job. "Paul's got a photographic memory," asserts Jeremy with a smile. "If I ever wanted to know which jets we used for those twin SUs in the car that we prepared for racing X years ago, I'd just have to ask Paul."

Both Paul and Jeremy were to be seen racing Sylvas in the various budget kit car series and Paul officially joined Sylva Autokits when they moved to Lincolnshire. "Premises for the kit building side were too expensive in Hampshire. I could still do the drawing work in Lincolnshire and Paul took charge of the kit side of things."

By far the majority of Sylva's advertising was by word of mouth, mostly within the racing fraternity, where class and outright wins were beginning to mount up. Many of these were scored by amateurs who hadn't spent the earth on their cars. It was (and still is) well known that the dynamic abilities of the Striker's design are the key to its track success.

Top: This neat cut away drawing of a Mk.2 Striker clearly shows the cunning front suspension set-up with its inboard coil-overs and rocker top arms. Above: A Striker working hard on the track.

No need for mega-buck racing brakes, titanium chassis reinforcements or outlandish aerodynamic devices.

Because the majority of Striker Mk.2 kits originally went to racers, though, the company had to be flexible in its approach to specification. The superb inboard front suspension had been well received, as had the twin longitudinal Watts linkages and Panhard rod for the live axle. Customers still needed all manner of different engine fitments for this lightweight flier. Everything from Mazda rotary to Ford Cologne V6, from Cosworth to Fiat twin-cam and Ford 1300 Kent to 2-litre Pinto SOHC etc.

In terms of kit content, the Striker Mk.2 package was simply a list of separate items, from which the race or road enthusiast could choose the essential components relevant to the proposed race series. This wasn't a 'complete de-luxe kit' for the family person or for the concours-building first-timer.

Bodywork front and rear sections in gel-coated GRP were designed to be sufficiently neat and cheaply and easily replaceable in the (common) event of a circuit ding. Plenty of attention was paid to the provision of the correct specification roll-over protection within the chassis design and also of various mounting point options for full harness belts.

Below: The Striker Mk.4, sometimes called the Sylva Phoenix or Clubmans, has simply dominated the kit car racing series since its launch in 1989. Bottom: Simple stripped out interior for this racer.

Years of abuse on the track were the Striker's testing ground. It was perhaps this insistence on catering for the close-knit racing community that kept the Sylva concern relatively small when the likes of Westfield and Caterham continued to rake in big money not only from their own racing clientele but from healthy sales to the general kit building public.

Neither Paul nor Jeremy were very interested in all the nitty gritty attention to presentation detail that went into making cars sufficiently refined and pretty for the beginner to bolt together with no worries. This wasn't their scene at all. They preferred to deal with the car-wise connoisseur who knew about problem solving and genuine functionality. The small Sylva build manual could never be described as a hefty volume for the clueless beginner.

In a way, it was a bit of an honour to become part of the 'Striker crowd'. The management would even discourage potential customers who seemed less than confident about their requirements and maybe a little woolly about the necessary techniques and principles of car preparation. That doesn't mean that Jeremy, Paul and co. were unapproachable. Quite the opposite. They were always extremely friendly and willing to impart volumes of knowledge with very little prompting. Even though Sylva had started to amass a small full-time staff towards the end of the 'eighties, the bosses were always involved in the production process.

Unfortunately, Paul had to leave for the south again at the beginning of 1990. That wasn't before the development of the short-lived Mk.3 Striker in 1989. This derivative featured a moulded tunnel section and outboard front suspension based on Vauxhall Chevette wishbones etc. The first Mk.3 featured a new location design for the Escort Mk.2 axle. The usual leading links were there but the long forward radius rods were replaced by a triangular A-frame with its apex at the differential base.

Subsequent models reverted to the longitudinal Watts linkage rear suspension but kept the outboard front end. Priced very reasonably, the Striker Mk.3 body/chassis kit found some 40-50 buyers, most of whom fitted Ford cross-flow engines. But Jeremy never much liked the model and continued to concentrate on making, and improving, the Mk.2 version – the car that was to carry on through the 'nineties.

Towards the end of August, 1989, the Mk.3 evolved into the Mk.4 Striker, with its fully-enclosed and more aerodynamic bodywork. The later Mk.3 suspension and

Above: The delicate Sylva Fury was based around a heavily modified Mk.4 bodyshell and was aimed squarely at the road user. Below: Even still, in typical Sylva tradition, it's a highly capable track performer.

chassis were retained. GRP parts manufacturer, Chris Appleby, yet another racing enthusiast, became an agent for Sylva in 1990 and struck on the name Phoenix for the Mk.4. Chris' involvement, both in terms of selling, building and competition driving, lasted until the first half of 1993, by which time the Sylva Phoenix had become a familiar sight on the track, with many victories to its name. Around 70 Phoenix and 270 Mk.2 Striker kits have been sold to date.

Whilst the pretty Mk.4 had been performing admirably on the track, with its perspex wrap around screen and low front spoiler, it was not the most practical road machine. Sylva's Jeremy Phillips was only too aware of this and in an attempt to grab the attention of non racing enthusiasts he set about redesigning a Mk.4 for the road. The Sylva Fury was the result, featuring full windscreen, doors and other modcons not normally associated with the Sylva marque. Still available today, it is now owned and marketed by Sylva's main southern agent, Fisher Sportscars (Sylva still produces the chassis). Sylva sold the Fury to make way its latest incarnation of the Mk.4, the new Sylva Stylus.

Sylva Today

Having established Sylva kit production facilities at the Dowlands Business Park works in Manby, near Louth, early in 1988, Jeremy Phillips has met with long-deserved success in the 'nineties. The Sylva Fury, with all-new chassis and super-attractive smooth body, was Sylva's first real entry into the general consumer's kit car market. It's been a real success since it first appeared on the cover of *Which Kit?* magazine's May 1992 issue, published in April of that year and the new Stylus looks set to continue that trend.

Together, the Mk.2 Striker, the Stylus and chassis production for the Fury make up the majority of Jeremy's workload, and recent developments to the Mk.2 have left the car equipped with special lower front wishbones, instead of the usual Escort Mk.2 track control arms, and with a slightly redesigned nose shape. It looks like the Fury body/chassis might even take over from that of the Phoenix (which is now marketed as the Sylva Striker Clubmans Mk.4A due to the fact that it now uses the company's Escort based rocker-arm front suspension) in terms of racing victories in the future.

Sylva's 3000 sq. ft. Manby premises now boasts two full-time laminators and two full-time welders, with Jeremy working there most days as well. That's not to say that the usually prolific Sylva think-tank has come to the end of the line in terms of new designs and ideas. With the prospect of tougher legislation aimed at kit cars in the foreseeable future, Jeremy still has a private room set aside for ongoing kit car design work...

Manby is situated right in the middle of wide expanses of Lincolnshire farmland. It has one of those small, rural industrial parks with no big companies to speak of, only small firms, mostly catering for regional demand. In short, it's a clean rural setting. Local roads are excellent and anyone driving across country will experience some exhilarating tarmac. There are far more NATO fighter planes patrolling the sky than there are Panda cars on the road, so Cadwell Park circuit isn't the only local testing ground. (Friendly fire hasn't been a problem for fast drivers as yet).

Sylva's small unit features a dedicated laminating shop, a tidy separate welding shop and a (not so tidy) general storage and kit collating space where the development/assembly work is undertaken. There's a small and cluttered office

Below: Sylva evolution - Star, Striker and Fury.

and the performance car fancier will be immediately aware of the amount of 'good stuff' lying about the place in tempting piles. A genuine Aladdin's cave for the racer-at-heart.

There are always a few interesting-looking engines in the development/assembly shop, along with a selection of new mouldings for all models, chassis and part-built cars. When this writer last visited the works on behalf of *Which Kit?* magazine, Jeremy's own track-racing 1300 Striker Mk.2 was waiting to go.

Needless to say, all the lads working at Sylva are sports car enthusiasts. Production volume is relatively small compared to the kit car industry's commercial giants and that really does mean that a lot of attention is given to each body and chassis. It works wonders when the people making the cars know that it's good.

It's the willingness to undertake a certain amount of tailoring to racers' needs that has created such a good word-of-mouth customer base for the Striker and other Sylva kits. Years of very valid racing know-how, exchanged between staff and customers, has also left Sylva with an excellent fund of kit building expertise and racing wisdom to pass on to new clients.

Whatever the modification today's customer has in mind, whatever the engine/gearbox fitment, whatever the subsequent cooling problem, Sylva will probably have sorted it for a past customer or will have the phone number of a customer who is willing to impart the information to another Sylva enthusiast.

Hence the enquirer will be given the knowledge that the currently trendy 16-valve twin-cam engine from the Astra GTE and a few other Vauxhalls can be converted to rear drive with the older Manta gearbox. The same effect can be achieved with the current rear-drive Carlton box. Vauxhall's 8-valve Carlton engine and box have also been used as an alternative to the ubiquitous Ford parts. The list is as long as your arm. In fact, the Fiat twin-cam with Mirafiori rear drive box appears to be the most popular option after Ford.

Although the Striker Mk.4A and particularly the Stylus, with their shared sleekness, are taking an increasing part of the Sylva production time, the Seven-ish heritage of the Mk.2 Striker still accounts for a good many sales. When performance-craving kit-builders, not of the racing fraternity, get wind of the Striker's incredible and gratifying road capability, it will really get the attention that it so richly deserves. What is it that makes the Striker so special? What are the benefits of such a prolonged history and production run?

Which Kit? **magazine's own Sylva Striker build project looked great with large 15" alloys. Soft top looks good on the car, too.**

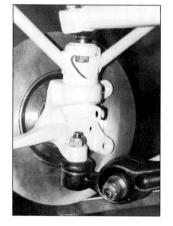

Top: Inboard coil-overs clearly visible on this rolling chassis. Left: Great location for the Escort rear live axle in the Striker. Right: Cleverly modified Escort front upright works well.

Current Models

As previously mentioned, the Striker Mk.2 is the only offering from Sylva which fits into the category of cars being considered in this hefty tome. With its low stance, cycle or clamshell front wings and strict two-seater spaceframe configuration, the Mk.2 leaves onlookers in little doubt as to its main purpose in life. It's one of the smaller cars in its category and this diminutive size, around 10'6" long and 4'11" wide, certainly helps to keep the structure rigid. This lack of bulk is also a much underestimated aid to performance driving – no good being quick if you're too wide for that gap...

At the heart of the Striker is Jeremy Phillips' multi-tubular chassis. It incorporates a selection of relatively small section steel tubes and a generous quantity of structural aluminium sheet carefully riveted into place after the chassis has been powder coated or otherwise rust-proofed.

Deep and very neatly triangulated side rail sections work in conjunction with generous front and rear bulkhead frames and a substantially cross-braced front suspension section to give a light and solid base for the suspension loads to work against. A roll-over bar is integral with the chassis and is available with extra bracing for race purposes. Available also, at extra cost, is a chassis specially made from lightweight tubes for the race track.

Once the alloy panels for floors, transmission tunnel, front and rear bulkheads, main body sides and dashboard etc. have all been fitted, usually at the works and for extra cost, not much of the chassis remains visible. The remainder is mostly covered by the 'wrap around' rear GRP body (with integral rear wings), the latch-on bonnet moulding (with one of many optional bonnet bulges) and the front cycle or clamshell wings. All of these GRP parts are available in gel coat colour finishes and can be quickly replaced in the event of an accident. More racing heritage, that.

Broadly speaking, the Striker Mk.2 uses Ford Escort Mk.2 donor parts throughout, but Sylva has seen to it that the bits which aren't 'quite right' for the job are made right. The Escort rear axle is relieved of its leaf springs and is treated to a set of new steel brackets positioned by the factory in the price of the kit.

Also included in the kit price is a set of five new tubular links to locate the axle in the chassis. Most manufacturers opt for a set of four short, nearly parallel trailing links, or radius rods, which reach from the rear bulkhead area back to special upper and lower axle brackets. Jeremy has rejected that approach in favour of twin longitudinal Watts linkages.

Left: Which Kit? magazine Striker built with 1600cc Fiat twin-cam and twin Webers. Below: Specially made leather seats looked great in otherwise simple interior. Below left: Note the slightly odd position of the gearlever for the 5-speed Fiat 'box. Worked well, though. Bottom: Compact dimensions and pretty styling of the Striker make it a popular option.

These feature one long trailing link each side of the chassis, mounted near the centre of the outboard side of the chassis and trailing back to the lower brackets on the live axle. Shorter leading links reach forward from the rear of the chassis to the top brackets on the axle. In addition to these, lateral location is assured via a long Panhard rod with its own specially triangulated axle mounting frame. Brackets

Above: This is Jeremy Phillips' own racer, powered by a highly tuned 1300cc X-flow. Note the new 'Jimmy Hill' front spoiler! Below: Hood is effective and looks good.

are also affixed to mount the pair of coil-over shock absorbers.

Essentially, the theory is that the Watts linkages effectively counter axle tramp and rear-steer, ensuring that torque is firmly transmitted to the ground via the tyres. There is also a dynamic downwards force applied to the axle, helping to create better traction under acceleration. All in all, this must rank as perhaps the best live axle location system ever fitted to a performance car. It works very well on road or circuit and has even managed to be an embarrassment to some expensive independent rear suspension set-ups.

Rear brakes are standard Escort drums and the handbrake mechanism is modified Escort. There's a Mini van petrol tank mounted within a protective rear frame underneath the floor of the diminutive rear boot area. Moving further forwards, we find that the Escort propshaft must be cut down and reassembled to the specified length by a prop specialist. The length will depend upon the engine and gearbox configuration used but due to the proximity of the gearbox to the differential (the engine is kept as far back as possible in the chassis) the prop ends up as a short one-piece item.

Even though the 1300cc Escort X-flow engine doesn't figure greatly amongst other performance kit cars, it's the most popular fitment for the Mk.2 Striker. Not only because of the keen following for the budget race series run by the 750 Motor Club but also because the lightness of the Striker lets you use it to excellent effect without huge cost. Remember that the 1300 Mk.2 Escort, and the 1300 Cortina for that matter, which both weigh substantially more than the Sylva, can bowl along at over 80mph with four passengers and luggage.

Unfortunately, the standard gearbox fitted to these 1300s offers the wrong ratios for a lightweight car. Most Sylva builders will be on the lookout for a gearbox out of a 1600 Sport Escort (the type with a bolt-on bellhousing). Alternatively, there's the choice of using the complete flywheel, clutch, bellhousing, starter motor and gearbox system from the 1.6 or 2-litre Cortina. These can be fitted to the Escort block without modifications, according to Sylva Autokits, and offer far better gear ratios. Having specified which engine, box and carburettors are to be used, the customer is given the option of the correct bonnet bulge, exhaust system (side pipe only) and, of course, engine and gearbox mounting brackets.

Sylva's inboard front suspension is one really curious bit of design and this race-bred technique has since found other fans in the kit car trade. The lower suspension link at the front is usually the Ford Escort Mk.2 track control arm. Instead of its usual location by the Ford anti-roll bar, a pair of special tie-rods has been used to triangulate the arms, still incorporating their large, central rubber bushes.

An extreme set of modifications is done to the Escort's integral McPherson strut/upright assembly, which leaves the builder with a simple standard sized upright. The bottom ball-joint is the Escort item but there's a new bolt-on upper ball-joint from a Chevette. The standard Escort hub retains its disc brake and the standard caliper also stays.

That top Chevette ball-joint secures the top of the cut-down Escort strut to something called a compression strut. This is like a top wishbone or arm which is pivoted at the chassis rail in the normal way but then continues inboard, where it is bolted to the top of a coil-over shock absorber. As the outer part of the wishbone or strut moves up, towards full bump, the inner part moves down and acts against the coil-over unit. This keeps the coil-overs neatly within the front nose-cone section and avoids the

Top: Sylva's own fibreglass seat mouldings are surprisingly comfortable. Above: Rev counter takes primary spot in the racer. Column mounted controls are a bonus.

dubious practice of putting a diagonal coil-over in an outboard position – acting upon the Escort track control arm and its ball-joint in an awkward configuration.

A recent development gives customers the option of a purpose-built set of lower front wishbones equipped with Sherpa track rod ends as their outer ball-joints. Either way, builders will use the Mk.2 Escort steering rack and column, an Allegro column extension piece, Escort pedals modified on exchange, a Viva non-servo, dual-circuit master cylinder and a radiator to be specified by Sylva for the engine fitted.

In most cases, the Escort wiring loom will suffice for all the Ford engine fitments usually chosen. There's also a selection of Maniflow exhaust headers and silencers to suit a fairly wide variety of power plants. Apart from donor parts, all of the items required for the build-up are listed separately by Sylva and their prices are very competitive indeed. There's even full weather gear and sidescreens...

Using a good, second-hand Ford 1300 X-flow engine and Cortina box, it is estimated that a complete Striker, with Ford 5.5" x 13" wheels, could be on the road for around ú3500 minimum. That's not expensive for one of the most exciting drives currently on offer from the kit car trade.

What's it like when you spend a bit more on it? Jeremy's personal lightweight Striker 1300 has a rather special engine and reputedly does very well on the circuits around the country. He also uses it sometimes to commute to and from work. Out on the road, courtesy of a break in the weather, it was quite a revelation to see just what can be done with a 'mere' 1300. In fact, there's quite a lot of effort invested in this particular motor...

It's been lightened and balanced, has 1100 Kent pistons for an 11:1 compression ratio, a Kent 244 cam, duplex chain, Mexico-valved head, Aldon points-

Heart of the Jeremy Phillips racer is this tuned 1300cc Ford X- flow which produces loads of laughs in the flyweight Striker.

type distributor, GT carburettor with various unmentionable modifications, light flywheel, competition clutch and even a small diameter crank pulley to slow down the water pump and avoid cavitation! The radiator is a special with twin cores and the cooling system has a Mk.3 Escort header tank plumbed in for extra capacity.

When an engine is moved as far back as Jeremy has done in the Sylva, there's usually a severe limitation on footwell length for the occupants. The problem has been averted for the driver as the engine has been moved over towards the nearside. The passenger, not needing pedals, is still assured of sufficient legroom.

There's no doubt that the X-flow Striker is a snug fit for this writer, at 6' and 15.5 stone! However, there's just enough room for all the necessary driver functions and plenty of lateral support when cornering heavily. Basic seat squabs, instead of the shaped seats fitted, would have freed up more valuable space. Width at the pedal end of the footwell was comfortable for energetic driving.

It must be said that the live axle is remarkably well controlled in this car. That rear suspension set-up provides grip and traction where most other live axle fitments, many of them very good as well, would have

given up the ghost to that 'unsprung weight' curse. Sylva's front suspension gives a superb lightness and sensitivity, with the overall handling characteristics registering at the neutral part of the scale. A superb balancing act for a rear drive, front-engined machine.

Accompanied by the side-pipe burble, the Striker driver is able to get the full benefits of a competent track racing machine which is tolerant of most road surfaces. Jeremy's own engine was just a bit peaky for pottering around in, though. Whereas most Ford engines start to get flustered at much over 4000rpm, this one didn't do anything until well past that.

Keeping it up at the 5500 mark, the little 1300 could be made to do all sorts of things that you wouldn't expect a really competent 2-litre+ production car to achieve. All this and superb fuel economy when you want it! No need for a fifth gear on the 1600 Escort Sport gearbox, driving the 185/60 x 13 Yokohama A001s through a standard 3.89:1 Escort differential.

Cornering poise and turn-in are frighteningly good and handling characteristics on the limit are excellent. Powering around corners and controlling

Above: Although some psychos have fitted Rover V8s into Strikers, the 2-litre Pinto is probably the biggest one could recommend. Below: Recently launched, the new Sylva Stylus is the company's most advanced model to date.

Stylus chassis, although similar to the previous Fury, has been heavily modified for the new car.

the rear end on the throttle may sound like journalistic cliches but it applies perfectly to this car. The Striker encourages you into it with conspiratorial keenness. It's pretty forgiving if you bottle out on the odd occasion but the limits of adhesion are so high in the dry that you really have to abuse the car to get into trouble.

Non-servo braking is precise and well-balanced, needing firmer pedal pressure than a modern production car with all of its power-assisted and ABS capabilities. All the old-fashioned driving niceties of feel, response and sensitivity come back to life in the Striker. Unfortunately, the confirmed hatchback or Sierra Cosworth fan won't necessarily like that aspect of it. Shame really.

There's hardly a test driver who dares to level any valid criticism at the Striker's performance road manners. So strong is the record of the car on the circuit and so tangible is its willingness to please that you'd have to be somewhat controversial to say that it isn't the bee's knees.

Perhaps the main criticisms of the Striker arise when the kit is viewed not as a specialist car, for road and track use by performance enthusiasts, but more as a package of parts destined to compete with other similar-looking offerings on the market. Many of the niceties of kit packaging have been dropped in the interests of functionality.

Leather trim and wall to wall carpeting? Nope. Wide-bodied, long footwell option? Nope. (Try the Stylus instead). Complete bolt-together kit with a yard-long list of comprehensive parts? Nope. 200-page comprehensive construction manual? Nope. Things have been left rather open-ended to cater for the serious range of options that Sylva's customers are in the habit of requesting. It's all still

down to personal service and recommendation.

Because the emphasis has been placed firmly on the road performance side of the car, some of the detail work has been rather neglected. Those bonnet catches might not be to everyone's taste. The basic interior specification won't win any concours competitions without a large amount of builder input. The GRP mouldings aren't exactly flawless and mirror-finished. Marketing for big time sales hasn't been one of Sylva's overriding concerns to date.

Even if Jeremy doesn't get to enter too many of the 750 MC races these days, due to pressures of work etc., he remains consistently dedicated to ensuring that the Sylva customers who do race are well catered for in terms of advice and parts. His customers tend to be very brand-faithful, and the low budget for the build means that they're often back for a new kit to try out their latest ideas on engines, 'boxes and suspension settings.

The Future

With the recent 'Jimmy Hill' nosecone shape and the optional lightweight chassis and lower front wishbones, Jeremy seems sure that the Mk.2's development and evolution are at an end. "I don't think that I'll make any more changes." Somehow, though, that seems a little difficult to believe. If there's something practical that helps to give the ever-popular kit a further track advantage, there's a strong probability that it will be incorporated in the end. Sooner rather than later.

Demand for the product as it is seems to keep Jeremy's inventiveness at bay. This doesn't mean that there aren't plenty of new ideas always appearing on the drawing board. Is there also a hint that Jeremy might move away from the strictly track-related types of car he currently produces? Who knows? Sylva Autokits is run as a very tight ship. It's never in the red and it always pays its own way these days. With the current recession and the prospect of new legislation limiting kit car production in the near future, it would be a little foolish to start investing bags of money on new and esoteric car designs straight away.

Although Sylva hasn't been as badly hit as some by the recession (it has done quite well, thanks very much) it is nevertheless a cautious company. Jeremy knows that the racing fraternity and its enthusiastic followers form the basis of its custom and they'll do well not to forget that – especially while cars like the MK.4A and the Mk.2 are still reaping rewards in various race classes.

A good future seems pretty much assured for the live-axled Striker Mk.2, though. Even if the Escort itself is becoming a rare donor vehicle, there are still sufficient stocks of parts to keep Sylva supplied for years to come. Mr. Phillips has definitely succeeded in designing a car with its own unique identity, and an increasing number of competitors is making sure that the Striker is doing what it has been designed to do.

It can be predicted that the company's venture into the 'general' kit car market with the pretty and more user-friendly Stylus will start to make them all a fair bit busier at the Manby factory. If further new models appear, then they might have to take over extra units on the estate. Such expansion does seem long overdue for a company which has had a strong following for over a decade and has managed to ride out the many storms.

It's refreshing to be treated to really personal service at Sylva Autokits and to be welcomed as a fellow enthusiast. It is a stark contrast to the big corporation image and a faceless-men-in-suits approach that mass-market success and the big time have brought to some kit companies. It might be selfish to say so, but there's no harm done to the customer if Sylva continues to operate on the relatively small and friendly scale it has reached in 1995. Sylva's success is typical of a seemingly British approach to car design ingenuity. You can do the job well with inexpensive parts and processes if there's a brain behind it all to say where everything should go. Simply throwing large volumes of money at a problem, adding natty technological bolt-ons and miracle computers, rarely solves the problem itself, even if the symptoms are alleviated. Is there such a thing as the 'thinking person's' kit car? Perhaps this is it?

Pretty from any angle, the Striker will continue to sell well to those enthusiasts looking for minimalist fun from a machine proven both on road and track.

Chapter 5

Westfield

A Brief History

Westfield Sports Cars is today one of the major players in the British kit car industry: arguably second

Chris Smith, Westfield MD, has seen the company grow into one of Britain's largest component car manufacturers.

only to Caterham Cars in terms of size and production output. Premises of around 27,000 sq.ft., production of some 500 kits and completed, type-approved cars every year and a multi-million pound turnover all add up to a highly impressive motor car manufacturing concern, but of course its roots can be traced back to the tiniest cottage-industry type of operation.

Back at the beginning of the 1980s, Westfield's founder, Chris Smith, ran a small classic car sales business from a lock-up in Armitage, West Midlands. Much of his spare time was spent as an amateur racing driver, a hobby he'd started in 1965 with a Turner. Success followed three years later in a self-built Sprite and co-driving a Chevron B8 at various tracks around Europe.

By the end of the seventies, Chris was to be found behind the wheel of a Lotus Mk 6, a car soon to be replaced by a second example which was rebuilt before being campaigned to victory in the 1970/80 AMOC Thoroughbred Championship. Was it this spartan little rocket and its amazing performance that laid a significant seed in the deeper caverns of the Smith brain? Seems likely, but nothing was to grow from that seed until another project had been created and concluded.

Westfield number one was to materialise in 1982, in the form of a Lotus Eleven replica, as the result of a casual remark made by a friend. In view of the vast engineering and mechanical know-how gained by his motor racing experience, it seemed utterly logical that Chris should attempt building cars rather than merely selling them. So the concept was drawn-up to include a light but very strong spaceframe chassis, MG Midget power and running gear, and a GRP body made from moulds taken directly off an original Eleven body.

Registered VTL 715, the prototype Westfield Sports worked well enough to impress all who saw it. "Shortly after I'd finished the car," remembers its creator, "a friend, car dealer Paul Matty, saw it and offered me 1500 sq.ft. of factory space in which to build some more. So I built the first batch of cars, giving Paul number two in lieu of rent, and we went from there."

At first, chassis were fabricated by Midas Metalcraft of Northampton but by the end of 1982 the work was being done in-house at Westfield's small factory at Netherton, near Dudley, West Midlands. GRP moulding work, however, stayed elsewhere on a sub-contract basis. Thanks to publicity in the US magazine *Road and Track*, a number of orders came from across the pond and Westfield Sports production moved steadily forwards. But the hand made and panelled chassis

Westfield's first sevenesque car followed the launch of the Westfield Eleven in 1982 while other models tried by the company included the Sports 2000 inspired Westfield SS.

was replicated. Called the Westfield Seven, the car used a multi-tubular chassis, Spridget power, the Spridget rear axle and many specially fabricated suspension components. Bodywork consisted of aluminium panels for the main sections and GRP mouldings for the bonnet, nose and four wings. If the 1984 kit price of the Seven sounded expensive at £2750 +VAT, remember that the package was comprehensive enough to include most suspension parts, windscreen, dashboard, steering wheel, seats, fuel tank, wiring loom, lights and weather equipment.

were time-consuming to build and the quality of the sub-contracted GRP tended to fluctuate. Another model was needed if Westfield was to progress.

Late 1983 saw the arrival of the new Westfield, a machine once again inspired by Lotus. This time it was the stark but sporting Lotus Seven Series I that

Early days with the Westfield Seven were fairly promising but soon came the desire for increased power, which led to the fitting of Ford crossflow engines. Next the search for an alternative rear axle led to the robust Morris Marina item, the extra width of which soon led to an updated Westfield which reflected the later Lotus Sevens.

By now, the Westfield Seven was becoming a quite different animal. As the Spridget basis was

Above: Westfield Eleven proved immensely popular, with over 100 having been sold by 1986. Below: Launch of the fibreglass bodied Westfield Sports SE was to change the company's fortunes for ever.

gradually phased out, the Westfield was using a choice of power units, Triumph Spitfire uprights and steering rack, Westfield wishbones and a Marina back axle on a specially made five-link location. Kits continued to be made with much the same specifications through until early 1986, by which time more than 100 Elevens and over 100 aluminium bodied Westfield Sevens had been supplied. Impressive enough, maybe, but Chris Smith was ambitious...

Reviewing the kit car market, Chris had quickly identified that Dutton's immense success was down to the pure affordability of a clearly low-quality kit. So the plan was hatched to capture Dutton's market with a far better product at a very competitive price. Enter the

Above: With a £995 kit price, the Sports SE was a runaway success. Right: This car went as far as to use an original Lotus twin-cam engine. Below: Westfield wishbones allied to Cortina uprights.

Westfield Seven SE.

The new car made its debut at the big national kit car show at Stoneleigh, Warwickshire, in May 1986. For a mere £995 plus VAT, kit car enthusiasts could acquire a multi-tubular spaceframe chassis, full GRP bodywork set (including bonnet, nose cone and front wings moulded as one piece), a collection of aluminium panels (for the floor, prop tunnel, dashboard, seat backs and interior sides), the windscreen and frame, four front wishbones, four rear trailing arms and various other bits of hardware.

All in all, it was an extremely tempting package. Add the engine, steering assembly, radiator, pedal box and rear axle from a Ford Escort, plus the front uprights, brakes and gearbox from a Cortina Mk 3/4, and you had a properly engineered kit car that performed well, handled superbly and didn't cost an arm and a leg. No wonder Dutton quickly began to feel the pinch.

By 1987, Westfield Sports Cars Ltd. was bubbling with full scale production at an impressive modern factory of 6000 sq.ft. capacity on an industrial estate at Kingswinford, West Midlands. The original Sports and aluminum bodies Seven models were still being offered, although these would tail off soon with final production numbers of 138 and 135 respectively. More in each case than Lotus had made of the originals!

A couple of Westfield models that didn't have quite the same impact were the SS and the Topaz. Inspired by typical Sports 2000 racers of the day, the

Early Westfields certainly looked the part and proved extremely popular. Trouble was, they looked just a little too similar to another car on the market.

SS of 1985 was aimed at the racing fraternity and used a light spaceframe chassis, independent front suspension and five-link live rear axle. Power was Lotus twin-cam mounted up front. Problem was that the car's ordinary styling failed to excite, with the result that only three examples were made.

The coupé bodywork of 1987's Topaz was similarly uninspiring. Displayed at the Stoneleigh kit car extravaganza in May that year, the 2+2 machine was Ford XR3i based with the CVH engine mounted midships and McPherson strut suspension all round. It became clear, though, that the car would be expensive to produce and would have a major task on

its hands to tempt people away from Toyota's hugely popular MR2, so the Topaz remained a one-off.

Apart from the disappointment of the Topaz – and, of course, the success of the Seven SE – 1987 was to bring upon Westfield one other significant event. It was the commencement by Caterham Cars, makers of the Super Seven, of legal action for infringement of copyright on both body shape and chassis design.

"We'd started building the early Lotus Seven Series I replicas in complete ignorance of any possible problems we might encounter," remembers Chris Smith. Caterham Cars' boss, Graham Nearn, wasn't exactly delighted with the coming of the Seven SE, either. Result of the court case was that both Westfield models were dropped amidst a flurry of extremely useful publicity for both companies.

A not inconsiderable amount of money was spent by Westfield fighting the action but the management was shrewd enough to gain plenty of press mileage from the situation. Overall, the company's name was brought to a much wider public through the magazine coverage gained, something it put to good use over the forthcoming months.

Replacing the discontinued models was the new Westfield SE introduced late in 1977. The model name sounded little different and the new car even

Above: The new SE with pre-litigation cars behind. Above right: Chris Smith loads up the old chassis jig to take to Caterham. Below: The new SE was to prove a complete winner.

looked very similar, but many detail changes had been made throughout. There were plenty of styling revisions, separate panels for the front bodywork, a fully revised spaceframe chassis and many mechanical changes. Also, an independent rear suspension system was designed and offered as an option in another model called the SEi.

The late 1908s were a period of remarkable success for Westfield. The cars' affordability and on-road dynamics were generating relentless orders, factory expansion was taking place and the marque was fast becoming the biggest name on the UK kit car scene.

The SEi's introduction was paying-off well. The car's rear end used Westfield's own cast aluminium uprights and differential casing housing an Escort diff unit which was available in various ratios. Along with the special wishbones and driveshafts, the arrangement was very effective and also enabled the

Above: Smart interior in the prototype SE. Where's the gearlever? Below: New design was inspired.

fitment of disc brakes on each wheel.

On the road, this model's performance surpassed even that of its earlier sisters: so much race-style chassis response and pure exhilaration were on offer that it was hardly surprising Westfield's reputation was gathering impetus fast. It didn't exactly hinder progress that kit prices were still remarkably low. £925 plus VAT was all Westfield asked for the SE body/chassis kit; the SEi was naturally higher at £1475 plus VAT.

The only discomfort about Westfield ownership until now had been a slightly cramped feeling in the cockpit for those of larger than average size, and this situation was dealt with by the development department at Kingswinford during over the winter of 1988/89. The outcome was another new model, the 'wide-bodied' SEi of spring 1989. This car, in fact, was exactly the same overall width as its predecessor yet cleverly incorporated three inches extra cockpit width. Helping to identify it visually were narrower rear wheel arches and three inches extra overall length (which allowed the cockpit to be longer, too).

Apart from improved comfort for driver and passenger, another benefit of the increased dimensions came in the engine bay, where there was now room for Ford's OHC range of engines. The range of possible power fitments, including the CVH unit, was quickly also carried over on to the standard SE and SEi models. The greater range of kits and various optional specifications simply meant one thing: Westfield sales went from strength to strength.

Yet another new model around this time was the revived and redesigned Westfield Sports. The company's original Lotus Eleven replica had continued to sell sporadically but by now supplies of Spridget donor vehicles were beginning to dry up. In an effort

to keep the glorious looking machine alive, it was given a widened, lengthened SEi chassis, CVH power and restyled bodywork which, in appearing to be an updated Eleven shape, contrived to lose its simple beauty and classic appeal. Needless to say, only a handful of kits were sold.

Not a *huge* quantity of the next new model was sold either, but that wasn't due to *any* deficiency of *any* kind on the part of car or company. Point was that the staggeringly quick, Rover V8 powered SEiGHT was a very special machine, indeed, and comparatively few kit car enthusiasts had the driving ability or sheer bravery to make full use of such a thunderous performer.

The first SEiGHT hit the streets in June 1991. Sitting proudly in its stiffened version of the regular wide-bodied SEi chassis was a 240bhp version of the 3.5-litre V8 engine driving through a 5-speed Rover SD1 gearbox to a Ford Sierra differential and wide 15" wheels. The outcome of a hard shove on this ferocious beast's accelerator was 100mph in a mere 10 seconds and a maximum of some 140mph.

"The main thinking behind the car," said Chris Smith, "was to create a very small, very high performance machine that, in the days of the seven-figure supercar, would provide supercar acceleration for not much money."

The SEiGHT certainly did just that; it was capable of out-accelerating a Ferrari F40 up to 120mph. Predictably enough, it immediately attracted widespread media attention and gained unreserved adulation. Every last motoring writer was gripped by the sheer thrill and explosive character of the car. "A Caterham on steroids," said *Autocar and Motor*; "One of the world's ultimate road cars," said *Which Kit?*

One important stipulation to buying a SEiGHT kit was that the factory would only supply a complete rolling body/chassis with all safety-critical work already carried out. That left the owner to source his own V8 and gearbox, cockpit trim, wheels and tyres etc. With the kit price being £4750 +VAT, total on-road cost could be around £8000, which represented genuine value-for-money for such awesome performance.

Of course, once bitten by the bug, Chris Smith and his development team suffered the odd niggling temptation . . . to make the beats go quicker still. 270bhp and 285lb ft of torque (at 4500rpm) were available from the special 3.9-litre Rover engine in the next factory demonstrator built in 1991. By 1993 the bhp figure had risen to a startling 330

Over the years Westfield has gradually put the car through a variety of approval tests. Top: Crash test. Above: Seat belt anchorage test. Below: The company's current 20,000 sq.ft. premises is impressive.

from a sensational TVR Power-built 4.3-litre version of the engine. Acceleration was now mind-boggling, to say the least, making a British kit car arguably the fastest road car in the world. The rewarding thing about the SEiGHT was that it could also be so docile in traffic and so usable at anything less than an all-out charge.

Mission achieved. Westfield had produced a brilliant sports car and quite rightly lapped-up thirstily all the superb publicity that went with it. Along with the maturity of receiving, in January 1993, the first ever Limited Vehicle Type Approval certificate for yet another model, the Ford Zeta powered ZEi (only available as a turn-key car), Westfield Sports Cars had unquestionably come of age: maker of both successful kit cars and full 'production' specialist sports cars.

Export sales have played a significant part in maintaining the company's stability over the last two years but kit manufacture still remains the essential part of the business. Relentless demand for the SE and

Above: Westfield's spaceframe chassis being welded on a jig that ensures each one is exactly the same. Left: Part build's are often undertaken. Below right: Front wings in storage. Below: Richard Smith oversees much of the day-to-day running of the company.

SEi in all their many forms has continued through the 1990s and Westfield remains at the top of the league in the kit car market.

That replica Lotus Eleven, closely followed by the replica Lotus Seven Series I, really started something. Caterham Cars might have legally squashed Westfield's Seven SE but the Kingswinford company has never looked back since. Genuinely affordable, top quality kit cars that provide full builder and driver satisfaction have unerringly made it a serious contender for the Caterham crown.

Westfield Sports Cars Today

Westfield's rise to fame has been the biggest success story in the world of British sporting cars and kit cars in recent years. From modest, race-oriented beginnings in 1982, Chris Smith's business has unerringly expanded to the current status of being the first kit car company to get a new vehicle past the recently invented Low Volume Type Approval regulations and tests. This means that the company has achieved production car status in a small way and that doesn't happen very often in this country.

A crystal clear perception of what the specialist car building public really wants is Westfield's basic recipe for success. It continues a tradition set by other historic British manufacturers which shows that effective performance cars for road and track can be built on a realistic budget, especially when the owner can make the effort to assemble all or part of the car.

Westfield's lightweight two-seater, with front engine and rear drive, was a quantum leap forward in low budget sports cars for the masses. Until the litigation by Caterham Cars in 1987, the live-axled, Escort-based Westfield was called the Seven but that name had to change, along with the design of the chassis and body. That wasn't before the Westfield marque had taken over from the ill-fated and rather shoddy Dutton Phaeton as the sports kit car for the masses.

New standards of chassis and body design, ease of construction and user-friendliness were combined with effortless sporting performance and brilliant handling, all at a reasonable cost. It was soon clear that enthusiasts were willing to pay something a little above rock-bottom price if the product was up to scratch. When the older Westfield Seven model was brought to an end after the court case with Caterham Cars, in 1987, the West Midlands concern had produced no fewer than 600 kits. The public still clamoured for more and even a complete redesign did not deter them. The product still fitted the bill nicely.

Then came the more recognisable SE, SEi and

This is a beautifully built standard body Westfield SE.

Top: Standard SE interior can be cramped for those on the larger side. Above: 2-litre Pinto engine provides plenty of power in the lightweight Westfield.

wide-bodied SEi models. These boasted completely new Westfield chassis and bodies, with the SE carrying on the traditional live-axled Escort base and the SEi embarking on a new road with the in-house IRS system also based on Escort axle components. A more in-depth look at the technical aspects of these kits will be undertaken in the following section. In brief, the SE, SEi and wide-bodied SEi still form the bulk of Westfield's output today. Various evolutionary improvements have been made to most of the cars, especially with the uprating of the SEi's rear suspension to Sierra differential with specially made half-shafts.

The most recent addition to the range of kits has been the V8 version of the wide-bodied SEi, called the SEiGHT. These are predominantly factory-built, thereby assuring a degree of conformity and also leaving a lot less work for the amateur builder to do.

The idea was to produce the fastest-accelerating thing around and the use of tuned Rover V8 engines has been spot-on in this respect.

In January 1993, the turn-key ZEi made its UK debut with its Ford Zeta 1800 16V twin-cam injection engine. It showed that Westfield Sports Cars had attained the development expertise and financial strength to undertake such a complex Type Approval task. It isn't a problem for the likes of General Motors, Ford and Toyota etc., as their budgets and design facilities are extensive. For a small company, just over ten years old, to move into production car manufacture from kit sales is quite an achievement. Ginetta Cars got there the hard way in the 'eighties with full Federal Type Approval for their G32 mid-engined model but it proved too much of a burden for them in the end.

Towards the autumn of its first year in production, Westfield had sold around 38 ZEi cars, the majority of these remaining in the UK. What about kit sales? To date, total SE/SEi sales (post-1987 models) amount to around 4000 units. Pre-1987 Westfield Sevens, known colloquially as pre-litigation cars, sold around 600 and the very earliest model, the Eleven, sold around 120 examples, many of which went to the 'States and Japan. That puts total cars and kits sold at not far off 5000. That's what you might call busy in kit car industry terms.

The company's current premises consists of two modern industrial units at the Gibbons Industrial Park. It's on the Dudley Road and is easily spotted to your right as you drive out of Kingswinford town centre towards Dudley. The main building, Unit 1, is around 20,000 square feet and houses the fabrication, stores, assembly and general administration facilities. There is an additional unit of 7000 sq. ft., catering for the laminating and other bodywork processes.

A relatively huge work force of 48 full-time and 3 part-time employees demonstrates the size of the Westfield concern. There isn't much idle space in these factories. Chris Smith's son, Richard, showed us around the works and described to us the various areas of specialisation. "We have four designers in-house and one full-time draughtsman." That's a big investment in research and development – meaning that the ZEi is probably just the first in a succession of production car projects to be undertaken by Westfield. Indeed, the new Cosworth powered ZEi 220 has recently entered production as the company's

This page and previous page: It doesn't matter whether it's a budget Caterham Classic or a top spec Vauxhall powered machine, Caterham quality abounds.

Above: Tiger Super Six SSI (foreground) features many styling and structural revisions over standard car (below). Both have received continual development.

The affordable and pretty Sylva Striker is all too often overlooked, yet its racing pedigree would put most other companies to shame.

This page and overleaf: One of the biggest operations in the kit industry, Westfield has an option to suit almost any customer.

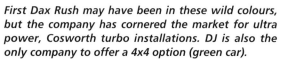

First Dax Rush may have been in these wild colours, but the company has cornered the market for ultra power, Cosworth turbo installations. DJ is also the only company to offer a 4x4 option (green car).

Robin Hood Engineering has dominated the budget roadster market in recent years with its Sierra based, stainless steel roadster.

flagship LVTA car.

Most of the production staff can turn their hand to each task in the factory, whether it is manufacture of the ZEi, the basic SE kit or any of the projects in-between. The main factory entrance leads you into the office and administration area. A duty receptionist then alerts the relevant staff member of your presence. A tour of the computer-strewn offices is ample evidence of the amount of paperwork involved in running a company of this size, with such a broad spectrum of production in the motoring field.

Much of the office space is open-plan and is kept tidy and efficient. At one side of Unit 1 is the main factory gate, a large entrance which leads the visitor right into the heart of the stores and kit storage/despatch area. The stores, to the left, is a two-floor collection of the myriad specialised parts sent out to Westfield kit

builders around the world. As expected, a heavenly collection of car building components is racked up in rows for easy access. Try to resist the temptation to reach for that credit card.

Once out of the maze of parts in the stores area, the wanderer can happily while the time away contemplating the various kits, part-built cars and race cars that can be found near the gate. Westfield do operate a post-build check-up service for kit car customers at extra cost. This is particularly good value as a customer will get 2.5 hours work by professional staff who correct small errors, advise on more major corrective work to be done and who also set up the suspension with the correct equipment. It's therefore likely that one or several customer cars are to be found in the factory.

"Most customer-built cars that come in are near-perfect," says Richard. "We might find some nuts and bolts installed the wrong way round but that's usually when someone has misread the build manual. If there is a safety fault on a car, we will sort it out before the car leaves the premises, although it may cost a bit more." A very sound after-sales service which many customers will take advantage of.

Another brightly lit and very busy section of Unit 1 is the fabricating shop. A handful of partitioned welding bays alongside one wall, and a large stock of steel tube and completed chassis in the central floor space, show just how popular the Westfields have become. Just ten years ago, things were very different indeed. Nowadays, skilled MIG welders produce tubular subframes on accurate jigs. These subframes are then assembled into chassis a little further down

Above: Chromed suspension wishbones are an attractive option. Below: SE is perhaps the best proportioned of all the various Westfield variations.

mounts for the Sierra A-type differential which forms an integral part of the Westfield independent suspension system. Others will bear the hallmarks of the ZEi and SEiGHT.

Elsewhere in the same section, SEiGHT and other part-assembled kits are being prepared by specialist staff. Not all customers want the most basic live-axled kit, even if it is the cheapest option in the range. "The SE kits out-sell the rest but there are still plenty of customers for the SEi and SEi Wide," says Richard Smith. The factory offers these cars as basic kits, rolling chassis kits or as complete kits with only four hours of work left for the builder. "Customers are very conscious of budget these days."

the line, different jigs accommodating chassis for different models.

All of the Westfields depend upon their chassis uniquely for structural strength and lightness and much of the factory production area is given over to this side of things. Obviously, the chassis is the largest single component of each kit, as the bodywork comes in several small parts, so it takes up the most room.

On closer inspection, it is possible for the outsider to distinguish between the different types of chassis stacked separately in the centre of the fabrication area. Some will have a relatively bare rear end to accommodate a live axle and others will have the

Wherever possible, Westfield follows the policy of keeping all production in-house. "We always get several quotes from external suppliers and then work out a price for producing the same part ourselves. It usually ends up much cheaper to do it here." However, some parts are shipped in. These include specially made propshafts, selected items of trim, windscreen assemblies, injection-moulded plastic components etc.

In an effort to avoid dealing with second hand mechanical parts, Westfield might recommend their customers to various sources for components that might otherwise be difficult to find. As their blurb says, they are still intent on offering a personal service to each customer, thereby trying to avoid that impersonal, corporate image.

There has always been a large options list with the Westfield. This adventurous hard top design has never really taken off.

"About 5% of customers ask for rolling chassis kits. 8% of production goes abroad." With an estimated 600 units produced in 1993 and 500 in 1994, it looks like the budget home car builder in the UK is still the most important customer for Westfield Sports Cars. It might be a while before demand for turn-key, Type-Approved vehicles outstrips that for kit-form cars.

Isn't it getting a little difficult to find the relevant rear-drive Escort components for the SE model? "It's not a real problem," asserts Richard. "We can still get the rear axles and, if necessary, we can get the rarer parts made for us. We can even get new Escort rear brake back plates from the original manufacturer." When you have purchasing clout, such problems as manufacturing new pattern parts tend to become mere inconvenience.

When the SEi and then the SEiW kits were introduced, it was, however, obvious that Westfield had kept up with the times in adopting a different

range of donor parts for some of their kits. Independent rear suspension also offers some performance advantages, especially for a road car – it also means that a sudden shortage of Escort Mk.2 donors won't be a problem for the factory. The SE, SEi and SEiW front suspensions share most components and use the Cortina Mk.3, 4 or 5 front uprights, hubs and disc brakes.

Ford's engines have always been the prime choice for Westfield builders. "We tend to stick with Ford as parts availability is good and there's still quite a lot of stuff available in the scrap yards. Even the Sierra is about eleven years old now."

The most popular engine fitment is currently the Ford CVH SOHC as fitted to front-drive Escorts. It's usually a front-drive unit, other than the 1800cc variant designed for the Sierra, but Westfield has shown its customers how to bolt it onto a selection of rear-drive gearboxes. A very sensible modification which is a benefit arising from Ford's level of standardisation in engine design. The Pinto range is the next on the list and the modified 1700cc X-flow Kent units are third. "Customers often choose the engine which is fitted to the factory demonstrator car."

Around 150 SEiGHT models had been sold by early 1995 and they qualify as the fastest Westfields on the road. In order to assure a high level of safety for these supercars, Westfield have taken it upon themselves to offer the kit only as a rolling

chassis, a complete car minus engine and gearbox or as a practically complete car with a 200, 270 or 330bhp engine and five-speed gearbox.

"This is to assure a good standard of basic equipment for these kits, especially where safety is concerned. We don't add on a labour charge for assembling the SEiGHT rolling chassis." Customers therefore do not have the option to use old and worn brake components etc. but the price is still kept as competitive as possible within the restrictions.

Because the SEiGHT has not been put through LVTA testing, it is still classified as a kit car and therefore, like the Caterham JPE, cannot properly be called a production car in the normal sense of the word. If it was a production car, then the 330bhp version could well be the quickest turn-key car ever made, in terms of acceleration to 60mph rather than

Below and right: The wide-bodied Westfield was an attempt to overcome the cramped cockpit of the standard car and was an immediate success.

top-end speed. Typically, a customer would pay around £25,000 for a top of the range version in complete form, with little construction work left to do.

One of the big advantages of the Westfield kits for the low budget builder is that the chassis kit and the body kit are available as separate packages, allowing the customer to spread the cost. At the end of 1994, the SE chassis kit was just £963.50 including VAT. A lot of the mechanical work relates to the chassis kit so the builder can get the project well underway before the body kit (priced at £505.25 inclusive for the same model) has to be purchased. Back this up with an excellent build manual and good off-the-shelf parts stocks and the prospect of building an attractive and quick sports car is suddenly within the reach of many.

"We've come to know the market place really well and I don't think that you can get better value for money. We've attracted the layman and now we aim to start appealing to a wider customer base. Next year, for instance, we will not be attending so many kit car shows but will branch out a bit." Richard Smith's reasoning seems pretty perceptive. Westfield believes that its post-1987 body shape change was a good thing. "You've got to be seen to be doing something new all the time. We rounded the body off but still kept the price down."

Isn't there a temptation for a company such as Westfield to come up with something completely new? Richard seemed to hesitate just a little before

Above: The SEI was Westfield's first independent rear suspension car using components from the Ford Sierra. Below: CVH engine installation has been a popular option.

answering that. A hint that something else might be in the offing before too long but no more information than that. "Radical styling changes polarise opinion. We're not heading mid-engined yet." That last point refers to the increasing amount of good front-drive engine and gearbox combinations available, which other kit car manufacturers are increasingly using as mid-engined assemblies.

"Customers tend to think long and hard before committing that kind of money. Some Westfield buyers have thought about it for four years or more before eventually placing an order. In fact, we still get a few people who ask for the old Eleven kit. It's no longer available, of course." That just goes to show that there is something to be said for keeping development pace even and steady, rather than jumping to a range of new, stylised extremes once a year.

Putting the ZEi through Low Volume Type Approval was a process which enabled Westfield to accumulate a large amount of knowledge in terms of the art of dealing with the Department of Transport and its associated agencies. It appears that the whole rigmarole cost in the region of £250,000 for the ZEi and only half of that budget was for testing purposes. There's a large amount of man-hours invested in consulting and adhering to the design regulations. The project was started late in 1989, taking three and a half years to complete.

As it happens, the ZEi looks rather similar to the kit-form models and there aren't that many components which are common to them all. Under the

bonnet, the Ford Zeta engine, with catalytic converter, means that the ZEi is compatible with the most modern emissions regulations. That bodes well for exports, which haven't been Westfield's forte in previous years. "The ZEi costs £14,450 inclusive in the UK and is only insurance group 12.

There are other things, however, that can be done to perk up demand and spread the word in the UK, even in the depths of recession. Since 1991 there has been a one-make Westfield race series organised by the factory in conjunction with BARC, using the RACMSA rules for such events. Even though there are special kit car races run by the 750MC, there are so many Westfield owners looking for track opportunities that there is ample interest in the one-make series.

Three classes are permitted in the 12-race series which runs for nine months every year. Amateur racers with a competition licence can take their mild or wild Westfield to the track and see what can be done. Kit car racing is still one of the cheapest forms of circuit competition for road cars and the public following is increasing rapidly. Obviously, budgets increase in the bigger classes and both Chris and Richard Smith have seen to it that racers of all types can be catered for by the factory.

Lightweight chassis and light alloy suspension parts are available, as are special aerodynamic body kits for the standard width SE/SEi cars. Racers will sometimes be using wheels up to 12" wide, as well as ABS brakes, Limited Slip Differentials, straight-cut gearboxes, rose-jointed suspension components and any number of variations in suspension geometry, easily permitted by the Westfield design. It's well worth watching. Even though factory cars do compete, they don't often take the laurels from other race goers. Is that policy or just coincidence?

Surely this is a good source of income for the factory, as cars must always get damaged at the races? "Not really," says Richard. "That's not why we sponsor the series." At the end of the day, the racing in the one-make events actually costs the factory a good deal of money, far more than the revenue from repair work and replacement parts. It's something that they do in order to stimulate interest in the marque. There's every possibility, with the currently high levels of interest in

racing, that more series might be in the offing. Perhaps something to encourage ZEi owners?

Needless to say, the light weight and excellent power to weight ratio of cars such as the Westfield are a good recipe for all kinds of motor sport. "There are plenty of amateurs competing in hillclimbs and sprints," claims Richard Smith. The very different requirements of each kind of racing format creates demand for new options and strange custom parts. "We're happy to try to sort out problems for racing customers." This is probably because the Smiths are themselves keen race drivers.

In just over a decade, Westfield Sports Cars has carved its name quite legibly into the list of British specialist car manufacturers. Why should this be such a unique case when there are so many good products originating from the many kit car companies? Several reasons become apparent. In

Below: Westfield interiors have continually improved over the years. This car features a 5-speed gearbox. Bottom: The company's fearsome SEiGHT is only sold with the suspension already fitted.

Above: The Rover V8 is a pretty tight fit but provides some of the most exhilarating driving possible. Right: Westfield hood works pretty well. Below: The author enjoys the shear violence that epitomises the SEiGHT.

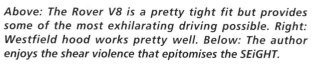

the first instance, the basic product appeals to a large proportion of the specialist car market. The styling essence is obviously a well-proven shape and the minimum budget is still very competitive with other companies who are trying to take the same route.

Unfortunately, it seems that other manufacturers in the kit car market have been just a little slow on the uptake or have decided to cater for a smaller niche. Chris Smith's razor sharp business acumen has correctly gauged the size and type of potential market for a value kit that delivers the goods and looks great. With a studied appraisal of what makes an amateur car builder tick, Chris and Richard have hit the nail right on the head. Sensible expansion and extensive reinvestment of profits into the research and development of new products has kept them popular.

There have been other relatively successful companies in the past but a tendency to avoid risks and to put real (ie: costly) development on ice has led to slow growth for them and some have fallen by the wayside as a result of this. Attracting new buyers into the kit car market is the key to success. When a company can convince a bank clerk, an accountant, a plumber, a student and other laymen that a kit car is realistically manageable project, then there is a prospect for big success. Much has been done by companies such as Westfield to bring the kit car to a wider audience. Engineers and mechanics are no longer the sole customer base for the British specialist car market.

There's still a long way for companies such as Westfield to go, though. If there is ever an end to this recession, the way seems clear to open up the kit car market to thousands more. There are plenty of sports car enthusiasts out there who might gaze longingly as a Westfield zooms past. They'll probably quail at the thought of wielding a spanner or screwdriver but do undoubtedly have the ability to complete a well-designed kit car. There's a good chance that some of these thousands could be converted to the ranks of the proud kit car owners in the UK.

Once bitten, forever smitten, as the saying goes. That doesn't mean that everyone has to buy a GTE or a Nova for kicks. Plenty of Westfield customers, taking advantage of traditionally good resale prices for their finished cars, have been back to the company for second or third kits. The younger kit builder might start off with a basic SE and might then work up to a tuned SEiW with the Astra GTE engine option as and

Cycle style front wings are proving increasingly popular, especially among racers. This is the company's first Vauxhall Astra powered demonstrator.

when the insurance becomes more affordable. Needless to say, these vehicles really can deliver plenty of driving kicks even with the smallest engines fitted.

What is it that has enabled the Westfield to bring so many new customers into the kit car world? We shall be taking an in-depth look into the principles and components of the Westfields in the next section. As a general theme, though, attention to detail is one of the biggest advantages over other companies. Not only is the build manual very professional but the huge proportion of technical enquiries answered by it, by the brochures and by the staff at the end of the phone are enough to convince many that there are no real nightmares waiting in the wings.

The Westfield Sports Car Club shows just how many amateur builders have been able to get their cars together just right, first time. At the kit car shows throughout Great Britain, visitors cannot fail to notice that the WSCC stand usually displays a vast quantity of cars. Sometimes 250 examples are there to testify to the buildability of the kits. Chances are that their owners will all have a pretty happy tale to tell. That's certainly one face of the kit car industry that proper investment and development will continue to nurture.

Current Models

Westfield's evergreen SE, as mentioned before, forms the base of the sales pyramid. It is the most direct descendant of the pre- litigation Westfield Seven and is the cheapest to build out of all the Westfield kits. All of the current models owe much of their design heritage to this car and to its immediate successor, the standard-bodied SEi.

This was basically one of the earliest comprehensive kits offering a relatively sophisticated and strong spaceframe chassis as well as an easy-fit, gel-coated bodyshell and commonly found donor parts. Various other manufacturers' kits have previously offered a good chassis, an easy-build body or commonplace donor parts but not usually all three

Below: Astra engine provides loads of power with only minimal tuning. Looks pretty impressive, too. Bottom: Specially made seats are a real treat for such a small car.

under the same roof.

Yet another obvious attraction to the SE was its superb road manners and widespread success on the track in the various kit car racing series. It certainly meant business, which was a big difference to being just another kit that could be put together by amateurs.

Predictably, a five-link live axle system is to be found at the back end, based around an Escort Mk.2 live axle which is modified by the factory in the price of the kit. Extra bracketry is provided and welded to the axle casing to offer locating points for four (trailing) radius rods and a Panhard rod. These special components are supplied in the basic chassis kit, along with metalastic bushes to be installed by the builder or at the factory. Escort rear drum brakes and handbrake mechanisms are retained.

Other features to be found at the back end of the car include a pair of coil-over shock absorbers, specially made Westfield fuel tank, a proprietary spare wheel holder, a small boot moulding and a roll-over bar which also doubles as a mounting point for the inertia reels.

At the front end, builders have the option of using the Escort radiator or one of several special Westfield alternatives. The tailor-made double wishbone suspension requires coil-over shock absorbers and uses the Ford Cortina Mk.3, 4 or 5 cast uprights, hubs, brake discs and calipers. There's also the optional light alloy hub/upright assembly to reduce the front suspension's unsprung weight. Westfield's steering system makes use of the Escort rack and factory modified Allegro upper and lower steering columns, as well as the ignition/steering lock.

The factory recommends that builders choose from the 1.1, 1.3 and 1.6 Kent X-flow engines, the 1.6 or 2-litre Pinto OHC units, the 1600 CVH OHCs typically from the XR2 and XR3 etc., the 1558cc Ford twin-cam, YB and BD Cosworths and the most recent option, the twin-cam 16V unit from GTEs and other 16V Vauxhalls.

These engines can all be fitted with suitable in-line gearboxes. In fact, the Kent engines cannot be used with their original gearboxes in unit with the bellhousing (if separate, then all is well). They will usually be fitted with a four-speed box from the OHC Cortina donor or with a five-speed Type 9 box from the Sierra or 2.8 Capri.

In order to achieve this, the Westfield build manual advises builders to use the clutch cover from a 1600 X-flow, the friction plate from a 1600 Pinto, the thrust bearing and clutch fork from the gearbox to be used and the standard flywheel from the engine in question. The thrust bearing sleeve may need shortening by 10mm. but this is otherwise a very simple bolt- together job. It's often adopted by other marques these days.

If the customer wishes to fit a standard Pinto

engine with a five-speed Sierra box, then the clutch components are reportedly standard for the engine and gearbox in question. The simplest way to fit a CVH engine in-line is to use the 1800 version complete with its five-speed gearbox from the Sierra range. If using a CVH engine from a front-drive Escort, Fiesta or Orion, then Westfield can supply a full conversion kit to bolt these units to the Ford four or five-speed in-line 'boxes. All this reflects the thorough way in which the factory has researched the ins and outs of building a small and specialised car using readily available parts.

Rather than leaving the amateur builder to sort out odd anomalies when building the car, much work has been put into a comprehensive manual and a selection of special parts which facilitate otherwise fiddly jobs. Specially shaped

coolant hoses, aluminium extension pipes, overflow bottles, electric cooling fans, optional wiring looms, engine and gearbox mounts are all available off-the shelf or are supplied in various optional kit specifications.

Whether builders use the standard downdraft carburettors or the sidedraft Webers, the GRP bonnet is usually cut to allow for air filter clearance and/or a moulded bonnet scoop. Exhaust systems for the popular engine options are supplied by Westfield,

Above: Westfield devised this wild bodykit in an attempt to make the car more aerodynamic. It has proved quite popular in racing circles. Left: Typical stripped out race interior. Below: The Westfield 11 has always looked good out on the track.

mostly in stainless steel throughout. They are all side-pipe systems requiring heat shields.

Moving a little further back along the car there's the specially made Westfield pedal box fitted with all pedals and supplied with a new master cylinder, clutch cable and throttle cable. In order to circumvent the complications caused by adapting the usually huge pedal assembly of a donor car, which will inevitably have an upright 'van-type' seating position, the factory has again seen fit to simply make their own components for the job. Again, nothing new in this principle but it's usually unheard of in a basic kit.

Westfield's SE chassis is a multi-tubular spaceframe built principally from 1" square mild steel tube as well as 5/16" and 3/4" round section tubes. Assembly is by MIG welding, firstly as a set of subframes and then as a complete structure on a main jig. It's a chassis which has been much imitated and, although it's not the stiffest available, it works very well without requiring huge amounts of labour time or large quantities of expensive materials. The

Kenneth Carlisle, minister for roads and traffic, presented Chris Smith with the certificate that allows the company to build fully built cars. Here both are sitting in the new Low Volume Type Approved ZEI.

main areas of strength are, not surprisingly, the bulkheads, tunnel and side frames, all of which are sensibly triangulated.

The SE's GRP body consists of gel-coated mouldings for the swept or cycle front wings, bonnet, nosecone, scuttle, boot and the main outer body sides and rear wing section, which are formed in one large moulding. It follows that the inner body is an assembly of separate panels, aluminium sheet in this case, which has to be drilled, sealed and riveted into place by the builder or at the factory for extra cost.

There is a wide choice when finishing the kit as to whether the builder uses donor parts or factory-supplied parts. Such things as the wiring loom, instruments, wheels and tyres might come from one or several Ford donor vehicles or can be ordered direct from the factory depending upon the available budget. Various specially made parts must be purchased from Westfield and some of these are not supplied in the basic kit specification.

Going up a peg on the list of Westfield kits, the prospective customer will find the SEi. This is a kit of the same overall dimensions as the SE, using basically the same body and front suspension formats. The big difference is, of course, the addition of an independent rear suspension system instead of the Escort live axle.

In the early days, customers could take their Escort live axles to Westfield who would remove all of the internal components and then modify and convert them to fit a new alloy differential housing, cast specifically for the job. This was, in effect, Westfield's own independent rear suspension set-up. However, the increasing availability of good second-hand Ford Sierra standard differential units and simple economies of scale have meant that most new customers will take the Sierra route. The factory has gone to the lengths of getting special half-shafts made up for the purpose, so as to avoid the job of cutting and shutting existing Ford items.

The SEi's chassis obviously receives a different rear section which incorporates a triangulated mounting area for the differential unit. Instead of twin radius rods and a Panhard rod locating a long live axle tube, the IRS (Independent Rear Suspension) car has been designed with wide-based twin rear wishbones. They locate specially cast alloy uprights and new hubs. The half-shafts, uprights and hubs are all provided in the basic SEi kit. Another example of no-nonsense problem-solving at a reasonable price. The customer will need Sierra rear disc calipers with a handbrake facility and a set of discs from a Mk.3, 4 or 5 Escort.

There is quite a high degree of adjustment in the front and rear SEi suspensions and the manual shows builders how to juggle the settings so that the car can be safely driven to either the Westfield factory or to a suspension specialist for proper castor, camber and toe-in checks.

Not all newcomers to the kit car scene are fully aware of the benefits of adjustable suspension settings but it's a little luxury that a specialist car can afford and that a lightweight flier really thrives on. The high-compliance, rubber-bushed and ultra-understeering modern production car has a knack of insulating the driver from the road environment. Something to be frowned upon by those in the know.

With the SE and SEi firmly entrenched at the forefront of the kit car market, it might have seemed tempting to keep it at that for a while. No, not really. Always one to spot a market niche, Chris Smith decided that there was sufficient demand for a new derivative specifically for the bigger and taller customers who still couldn't fit into the standard Westfield cockpit.

Along came the SEi Wide. This essentially represented a completely new departure, as it resulted in another chassis redesign and a new set of mouldings. Whereas much of the SEiW's mechanical basis remained the same as those of the SEi, there was at least another 3" of cockpit width and 3" extra footwell length. That succeeded in making this particular kit the most capacious of its ilk, permitting unprecedented access to a small sports two-seater for many large-sized drivers.

Styling compromises were made and some of the Westfield purists, who have often mourned the loss of the pre-litigation cars, voiced distinct disapproval of the SEiW's relative ungainliness compared with the old car. Westfield are unrepentant. "We think of the car as our unique and original design now," says Richard. An indication that things weren't necessarily always like that.

Despite the fairly obvious styling and proportional difference incorporated into the new SEiW, it has still managed success in sales terms and has even lent itself to development of a newer model. The major differences from the SEi, apart from the obvious body/chassis changes, include the use of the Sierra handbrake mechanism, special windscreen and frame, propshaft, exhaust system and roll-over bar etc.

This writer, at 6'1", can testify to the internal size of the SEiW. With adjustable, sliding seats fitted, there's enough seat runner movement for very long legs. If the seat is moved all the way back, it's nearly impossible to reach the pedals. Shoulder width is generous and that makes it much easier to cope with a harness type seatbelt if the builder chooses that option.

No wonder that the SEiW was chosen as the basis for the evolutionary SEiGHT model. This has been Westfield's record- breaking flagship. In essence, it's an SEiW body/chassis kit with all of the modifications necessary to turn it into a home for a modified Rover V8 engine of 3.9-litre capacity or more. The increasingly powerful demonstrator SEiGHTs have consistently broken acceleration records in this country.

Caution has been the key word in releasing the SEiGHT for public consumption. Westfield Sports Cars didn't want to allow potential customers to get hold of a basic kit and then produce some kind of unstoppable monolith by economising on the brakes and other safety equipment in order to pay for the engine. It's also known that there are always more complications with a V8 than with a four-cylinder unit when the builder is trying to squeeze it into a small space.

To exercise a greater level of control over the build standard of SEiGHT kits, Westfield decided to offer

Westfield spent several years developing the ZEI. Note how the front of the wings has had to be changed to shield the front wishbones.

Top: ZEI interior is particularly sumptuous for such a machine. Above: Ford Zetec engine comes complete with catalytic converter.

them only as a rolling chassis kit with many brand new components fitted at the factory. The builder, at most, would have to supply and fit the engine, gearbox, engine bay ancillaries, bodywork and cockpit fittings. Obviously, the factory quotes for higher stages of preparation if the builder can afford it. In early 1995, the price of the rolling chassis SEiGHT kit was £3950 inclusive of VAT. With Westfield supplying V8 engines from 200 to 330bhp, along with limited slip differentials, chrome-plated suspension and roll-over bar, optional leather trim and a stainless exhaust system, the SEiGHT certainly rates as the most expensive standard Westfield – and the quickest.

Even though it's not the top performer, the production ZEi must rate as Westfield's flagship product – at the top of the pyramid. The Ford theme continues with this independently suspended vehicle but modern emissions regulations and the ins and outs of LVTA have meant that an up-to-the-minute engine choice had to be made. It had to be an engine that would be affordable and available for a good long time to come. No good Type Approving a car with a good engine, only to find that the engine in

question becomes extinct within a year or two.

Ford's Zeta twin-cam, the 1800cc, 16-valve version that sets out to take on the Japanese and the other Europeans at their own game, was Westfield's wise choice. Good performance, good price, affordable spares and adaptability for the job in hand have all meant that Westfield stuck with Ford yet again.

Plumbing the engine and its catalytic converter in under the bonnet was one of the tricky engineering tasks undertaken by the car's designers but they have done it all neatly, getting new components manufactured where necessary. An initial VAT-inclusive price tag of £14,687 had been reduced to a mere £12,999 by the end of 1993 and by early 1995 had risen again to £14,450. Presumably the recession-bound new car market has finally begun to pick up. The ZEi first became available in the UK on the first day of January, 1993 and by early 1995 around 140 examples are said to have been sold, with several of these going to Japan and a very few others leaving these shores.

At a glance, the ZEi does resemble the SEiW kit version but closer scrutiny will reveal all kinds of styling and detail changes, many of which were instituted in order to pass the LVTA tests and specification requirements. It's a more swooping and rounded body shape, especially up front, and there has been plenty of new work done to make the screen, interior trim, seats and weather gear a lot more sophisticated than the traditionally hard-nosed, all-weather sports car enthusiast might need. This is a car that has to appeal to production car owners looking for a fun chariot. They might be only dimly aware of a kit and specialist car industry in the UK and would certainly never wish to heft a spanner.

"We are setting up a specialised dealer network to distribute the ZEi," says Richard Smith. "We're looking for dealers in Germany and Holland as well." Typically, prospective ZEi dealers will already be sports car specialists in their own right, so the Westfield will be rubbing shoulders with other cars of suitable road-going potential. "In Germany, for instance, a car like the ZEi is very cheap." That's a reference to the excellent exchange rate advantages enjoyed by British exporters since Black Wednesday and our rushed exit from the ERM.

It could well be that second hand high performance production cars are becoming cheaper and cheaper as insurance companies heap on the long-overdue penalties, especially against younger drivers. Along with a generalised spending shyness, this quite good availability of hot hatches, MR2s and MX5s may have slowed down the initial sales of the ZEi. Unfortunately, those who have not experienced spaceframe sports two-seaters don't really know what they're missing in terms of pure performance. It's difficult to spread the gospel in words alone...

While the glamour and newness of becoming one of the latest British production car manufacturers might lure sympathies away from the kit car world, it looks like Westfield are under no illusion as to which side their bread is buttered. It will be a while yet before the ZEi has paid its own way in the world and until then, the kit side of things, based mainly on SE, SEi and SEiW output, is the big earner.

The Future

Because most of the manufacturing processes for the ZEi have been well integrated with those of the Westfield kit cars, both on the chassis and body side of things, there has been little dramatic upheaval in the everyday running of the business. Obviously, there have been many refinements to the system to get it all coherent. Any real changes would have to be substantial to be noticed by the infrequent factory visitor. When seeing a kit car manufacturer's premises reach the kind of size attained by Westfield over the last decade or so, an impression of solidness, of continuity, is natural. Big concerns like this are generally more likely to last than a shoddily run and untidy workshop-based project.

Is the move towards a production car something which has been spurred on by the prospect of new and more restrictive laws relating to kit cars? Richard Smith is rather less than resigned to the advent of a new Super-MOT for kits or other drastic restrictions on kit car specifications. In fact, it looks like this country will benefit from the simple amateur build exemption from Type Approval, and a standard MOT for kit cars, for the foreseeable future. "The government will probably consult the kit car organisations such as the SCMG and STATUS before making their final decision. The members will throw out any wide-ranging limitations."

"If greater restrictions on kit cars do come into force," Richard reminds us, "our experience with LVTA testing for the ZEi means we can design kits with catalytic converters, fuel injection and all that. We wouldn't need to worry as much as some others." Westfield certainly won't be one of the companies left on the rocks if the UK government suddenly decided to take a tough new stance on enforcing revised Construction and Use definitions for kit cars built by amateurs.

"The industry might be whittled down to a handful of companies. For instance, cars with twin Webers probably won't pass emissions tests." Headlight heights, external protrusions, seatbelt mounts and other specifications will certainly take their toll amongst the manufacturers of the smaller, sporting kit cars.

What about new models? A wall of silence always greets such questions at Westfield. It usually means that of course there's something in the pipeline (there always is) but we're not going to tell you. The financial burden imposed by the development of the ZEi must have been pretty telling and the most likely new products could well centre upon different versions of the ZEi for the production car market. Already we have seen the introduction of the mighty Cosworth powered ZEi 220. The number relating to the performance output from the turbo engine. It has received rapturous reviews from the mainstream motoring press and is in many ways very different from lessor powered standard ZEi. Might Westfield look for something with an even beefier engine, for example. What about a V8 model in turn-key form? It would be pretty expensive but very quick as well – something that can turn a little-known cult car into a top seller.

As far as the kit car trade is concerned, Westfield keeps its eyes open for new possibilities. It is inevitable that the kit packages themselves will be subject to the usual stream of slight improvements, especially when new components become available or new engine/gearbox conversion kits reach the market.

Latest changes to the company's kit packaging has been the introduction of the SP, SPi and SPa models. Aimed at providing the kit builder with every last nut and bolt required to put a car onto the road, the SP range has been incredibly competitively

Cosworth powered and approved ZEI 220 is quite a different beast to the recently launched budget SP.

packaged. The basic SP is based on the standard Westfield SE chassis and body and uses only new or fully reconditioned components. From the package the builder can assemble what can be best described as a stripped out SE fitted with either a reconditioned 2-litre Pinto engine or 1700cc X-flow unit (both with 4-speed gearbox). The SPi offers much the same on the independent rear suspensioned SEi body/chassis unit while the SPa is a semi-completed SPi requiring only the minimum of assembly work by the builder. Prices at the beginning of 1995 were £4999.99, £5999.99 and £9999.99 for the respective models.

Will they go in for an entirely different type of kit car in the future? That suggestion isn't met with total incredulity but there's no evidence that the company has its eye out for any particular product already on the market. The Kingswinford works certainly has the buying power to snap up something that could be turned into a profitable second string. Because demand for the SE and SEi derivatives has been so strong, though, there has been seemingly little point in going after something else which can't promise sales anywhere near current Westfield levels.

Given a continuing and healthy level of output for today's range of offerings, it must be said that Westfield Sports Cars is one of Britain's few hopes as far as emergent new production car manufacturers are concerned. The ZEi has been a sensible starting point, benefiting from the company's considerable expertise in making cars of this type, but there are undoubtedly many more ideas forming in the minds of the bosses and designers at Westfield. Something to appeal to a much wider market next? Time will tell.

Cosworth power gives ZEi enormous potential but lightweight SP with 2-litre Pinto is no slouch. Which ever you choose will provide plenty of thrills.

Chapter 6

Robin Hood

Like so many men who run specialist kit car companies, Richard Stewart, boss of Robin Hood Engineering, is a true individual and something of an eccentric. Would the boss of Volvo or Skoda live in a converted church shared only with a pet polecat called 'Sid' and a basement full of rare old cars? Another typical trait is endless creative ability born, in Richard's case, of necessity.

"I came from a poor family and at Christmas time my parents couldn't afford to buy me new toys. So I quickly learnt to be an inventor and make my own!"

Born in Scotland, Richard was five years old when the family moved to Nottingham. Not the greatest lover of academic studies, he had started out in the motor body repair trade by the time he was nineteen. Significantly, he moved straight into working on early saloon cars of monocoque construction: models such as the Hillman Minx and Morris Minor.

"This construction type was in its early stages for mass-production cars and so a lot of new problems were being created. I was fortunate enough to be in almost at the beginning of engineering and repair learning with monocoques, and thus gained terrific experience in modern car body design. This was really valuable when I later started to build Robin Hood monocoques."

Success in the trade came easily to Richard. Running his own business from rented premises in Nottingham, he was soon specialising in 'classic' car repair and restoration. An avid sports car enthusiast, his taste for special cars wasn't restricted to working hours. Regular everyday transport involved such desirable machinery as an E-type Jaguar, Corvette Stingray, Aston Martin DBS and various Bentleys.

It was a beautiful Bentley S3 that Richard sold in 1971 to provide funds for the purchase of the workshop premises which he still occupies today. Situated in the Sherwood area, north of Nottingham, the rambling building had previously been a Wesleyan chapel, and its many different rooms of varying sizes were ideal for a growing motor body repair specialist – plenty of space for several workshops and lots of storage room, too.

Predictably enough, it wasn't long before Richard's creative instinct began to demand expression. Amidst the clatter and clunking of the day-to-day bread and butter work, there began to form a fairly outrageous (for the day) strain of 1962 Ford Anglia. Such mundane family transport had never for one moment been conceived with even an inkling of Jaguar 3.8-litre straight six power but there, in a corner of the old chapel, was Mr Stewart making absolutely sure the strange marriage was

Just some of the Robin Hood team outside the company's Nottingham base. Main man Richard Stewart in the light shirt.

consummated. The beast used Jaguar suspension, too, including the wire wheels. It was called the Janglia and charged on to become quite famous in hot rodding circles.

As time passed, several other body conversions were schemed and carried out by Richard's ever-fertile mind. They were mostly pick-ups and included one particular stunner, a 6-wheel truck based on a 1974 Escort. By this stage the company was not surprisingly just as well known for its conversions as its repairs. Small surprise, then, that the boss's favourite reading came from American hot rodding magazines.

It was upon the debut of the company's first 'production' car (more a conversion than a kit) that the Robin Hood Engineering trading name came into being. "It was in 1979 that we slipped into the kitcar business," recalls Richard, "and it was almost by mistake. I very badly wanted a Ferrari Daytona but hadn't got the £50,000 they cost at the time. So I decided to build my own version, using the only method I knew: by cutting a Rover SDI V8 into bits and welding it back together with new panels to create the Daytona shape."

Offered for sale as a Rover conversion which could be carried out at home by a skilled d.i.y. enthusiast or completed by Robin Hood to turn-key stage (prices varied from £8000 for a full home-assembly kit to around £20,000 for the finished job), the RS Daytona was in regular small scale production during the early 1980s. By 1987 an optional version was available using the Jaguar XJ6 or 12 as its donor, the whole concept now clearly making more sense than ever. The original Ferraris had rocketed in price to anything between £80,000 and £120,000, depending on condition,

First real kit car work involved Ferrari Daytona replicas based on various different donors from Rover Vitesse to Triumph TR7.

while a Jaguar V12 powered RS replica provided lookalike styling, the same image and very similar performance, all for a fraction of the cost.

A small number of RS Daytonas were even built around the Triumph TR7 sports car but these more affordable versions came at the end of the marque's line. "It was getting more difficult to sell the Daytonas," Richard remembers, "because people were demanding better detailing and more perfection; they wanted to pass-off their cars as real Ferraris."

Time to move on. With something approaching 60 Daytona conversions sold/built, about two thirds of them on Rovers, Robin Hood's master of imagination was scheming his next plan. Lying around the yard of the Sherwood premises were plenty of old TR7s which had been bought in anticipation of the RS Daytona conversion project carrying on unabated. It didn't take Richard Stewart long to decide what to do with them...

At the big Stoneleigh kit car show in spring 1989 was launched the forerunner of the Robin Hood S7 you know so well today. Billed at the time as 'The Latest Chapter In The Evolution of The Super Seven' (not exactly to the pleasure of Caterham Cars), the all-new model was called the RS TR7. With kit prices starting at an affordable £995 +VAT, it was hardly surprising that the car caused an immediate buzz and soon started to sell well.

The inspiration for Richard's latest creation was clear, the RS TR7 adopting an original-style sevenesque approach to its design and construction. Under the functionally pretty body was a true spaceframe chassis (not unlike Caterham's) fabricated from square section steel tube. Body panelling was in brightly polished stainless steel for the bonnet, side section and rear end and in self-coloured GRP for the nosecone and wings.

From the TR7 came the majority of the mechanicals: the 2000cc aluminium head engine, gearbox, steering, driveshaft, complete rear axle and front stub axles, the latter working in conjunction with Robin Hood's own wishbones and special coil springs. With the donor car bought for around £500, it was claimed that the completed RS TR7 could be on the road for little over £2000.

It was the sort of budget that raw sports car enthusiasts liked – and were sorely tempted by. The new model was quickly in demand, successfully launching an exciting new era for Robin Hood Engineering. True, there were initial legal wrangles with Caterham Cars over design and copyright but these

plus VAT, no vital extras (apart from the donor car) were needed to complete a sensational looking sports car. Better still, the Dolomite came with a range of engines wide enough to suit every taste. There were 1300, 1500, 1850 and high-performance 2-litre Sprint options: everything from mild to wild. Not surprisingly, it wasn't long before the new S7 was in great demand.

Such popularity could only be enhanced by the availability of a Ford donor vehicle, and so it was that early in 1991 the Robin Hood marque finally sealed its success with the announcement of an additional Cortina Mk 4/5 based version. From that point on, there would be no looking back: the S7 would soon establish a reputation as one of the best known and most popular kits on the market.

Throughout its production, the Dolomite based S7 was always available in two forms: with the stainless

soon faded in favour of the Nottingham company, leaving the Robin Hood marque a clear path towards a deserved entry in British specialist sports car history books.

Key to the immediate success of this forerunner to today's Robin Hood roadster was its enticing combination of classic sevenesque image, low on-the-road cost and larger size (and thus more spacious cockpit) than comparable Caterhams and Westfields. The only problem laid with the cost of actually manufacturing the chassis: the complex and extremely strong spaceframe was really too expensive and time-consuming to make for what was essentially intended as a 'volume' production kit.

The ever-inventive Mr Stewart soon had the answer for this problem: a new model (indeed, the first to be called Robin Hood S7) packing the powertrain and running gear from a Triumph Dolomite into an all-new and somewhat unique monocoque body/chassis unit. Why unique? Because it was made entirely from stainless steel – a first for the kit car industry and, indeed, a first for the car industry, period.

Launched early in 1990, the new S7's revolutionary construction was created with the help of computer technology, which guided the laser-cutting of the stainless steel panels before folding and welding them to form an extremely robust assembly which would never be affected by the dreaded rust. By the time the process was complete, all interior and exterior body panels were in place. As virtually everything else required to complete the car, bar the donor vehicle parts, was included in the kit package (a leather interior was chucked in for good measure), it was clearly a sensible buy for the first-time builder.

Again, kit car enthusiasts were not slow to recognise a good deal when offered one. Even though the monocoque kit's price was now £2300

Above: You might recognise the alloys. First Robin Hoods were based on Triumph donors. Below: Triumph clocks certainly looked the part in the simple interior. Bottom: Familiar Triumph front suspension.

steel monocoque or optionally with the old spaceframe chassis. For a while, this situation remained unchanged for the Cortina based version, mainly because of problems with outside suppliers in getting the revolutionary monocoque into full series production. Indeed, for one difficult period, lasting several months through 1992, the company found itself unable to accept further monocoque S7 orders while it cleared a rather large backlog.

Above: Very soon Robin Hood was into volume production. These are Triumph based spaceframes. Below: Robin Hood S6 had this slightly odd barrel rear body design but was nevertheless quite pretty.

Once this was sorted, however, the popular S7 went from strength to strength. Looking at the company's direct and aggressive marketing policy and the unusually comprehensive nature of the kit packages, it was perhaps easy to see why enthusiasts were tempted to the Robin Hood in such large numbers. The message was short, sharp and sweet: great kit value, one donor, an easy build, few necessary extras and a low on-the-road cost for an immensely strong, rust-free, good looking and practical sevenesque sports car.

Various S7 derivatives were devised by the ever-fertile imagination of Richard Stewart through the early 1990s, including the mildly restyled S5 and S6. About 40 kits of the latter model were made: it was easily identified by its rounded, barrel-like rear end. Another S7 derivative was the Cheven – yes, a Vauxhall Chevette based Robin Hood. In fact, it wasn't an 'official' factory model, the project being schemed-out, engineered and assembled by a very keen customer, Chris Hind.

Using a specially fabricated stainless body/chassis unit, the Cheven was a smaller S7 than the wide Cortina based car and was for some time a genuine contender for production. But although it debuted on Robin Hood's stand at the Kit & Performance Car Show at Donington race circuit in October 1993, the Cheven was destined to remain a one-off.

The same fate sadly awaited another rather more sensational Robin Hood, the outrageous Jaguar powered S7 V12 of early 1993. This thunderously quick machine was built by Richard Stewart specifically to test to the limit the already proven strength of the Robin Hood stainless steel monocoque. If anything would pinpoint any weakness, it had to be the massive power and torque of Jaguar's mighty V12. The monocoque was well up to it, though. Richard used the car personally on a daily basis and pushed it hard whenever possible – with never a problem. But he insisted its status remained strictly as originally intended, as a one-off testbed.

It was possible a few well-off, serious performance freaks might have wanted the S7 V12 to indulge their whims and fantasies but there was no way the model would fit into the growing 'mass-production' school of thought at Robin Hood Engineering. It was unquestionably the straight-forward Ford based S7 which shone through as the Robin Hood that everyone wanted. Not surprising considering the company's approach to marketing. The message was quite stunning value-for-money: "Be on the road for less than £1900," said the advertising. Ambitious, perhaps, but quite possible to achieve if the builder was extremely frugal in his approach.

Kit production figures through 1993 were extremely impressive considering the specialised nature of the industry, with sometimes as many as 20-30 customers collecting their d.i.y. dream machines each week. Robin Hood Engineering was now, without doubt, one of the major names in the kit car industry.

Further consolidation of this standing came with the launch of the new Sierra Seven at Stafford's Sports & Replica Car Show in March 1994. The latest, cleverly devised package from Richard Stewart's ever-imaginative mind met with instant success, and it wasn't difficult to understand why. With components bought in bulk, kit production set at up to 20 units per week and profit margins trimmed to the bone, the new Ford Sierra based Robin Hood debuted with an astonishingly low comprehensive kit price of £999 plus VAT.

The best value-for-money kit car in the world? Probably. What customers got for their money was a

The most opulent interior you are likely to find in any sevenesque car. S6 never quite gained the same following as slightly larger Cortina based S7.

package absolutely loaded with components. Starting point was the latest Robin Hood zinc-coated mild steel body/chassis unit with panels pre-fitted, GRP wings and nose cone, complete windscreen assembly, all lights, grille, special suspension components, fuel tank, brake pipe set, stainless steel exhaust system, free-flow manifold, full interior trim kit, seats, radiator, steering wheel and much, much more.

The all-independent Sierra Seven really was a quite extraordinary bargain. Only a Ford donor vehicle was needed to provide the builder with every last part required to complete his super-budget

Cortina based S7 is now no longer available but has provided the bulk of Robin Hood's sales up until the launch of the new Sierra based car.

performance roadster. It was even possible to get a car roadworthy for around £1500! No wonder that at the next kit car show that year, the major event at Stoneleigh, the Robin Hood stand was inundated and signed-up nearly 50 orders over two days. An outstanding performance.

This remarkably healthy sales situation continued throughout 1994, by the end of which no less than 500 Sierra based kits had been manufactured and supplied. This figure surely beat by a long way any previous sales performance by a newly launched car.

But 1994 wasn't all roses. Caterham Cars, makers of the original Super Seven, had always been rather less than delighted at the very existence of the S7 and there had been various legal exchanges over Robin Hood's use of that model designation. Following more litigation, the Nottingham company finally resolved late in the summer of 1994 to quit using the S7 name. Furthermore, it agreed never again to promote the Robin Hood marque with a car painted in BRG with a yellow nose cone and longitudinal stripe in the style made famous by the Caterham car. Pettiness? Hmmm...

Another company not entirely happy with Robin Hood was the mighty Ford. At about the same time as the exchanges with Caterham, Ford wrote a nice

friendly letter to Richard Stewart asking him to kindly refrain from calling his car a Sierra Seven. Obviously, no-one squares-up to the likes of Ford and gets away with it. Richard didn't even consider it.

From autumn 1994 on, the famous S7 was renamed the Robin Hood. More importantly, from this point onwards the car would only be based on Sierra donor parts. This decision made plenty of sense: Sierra bits were more suitable for the Robin Hood in many respects, they were much more modern than Cortina parts, and they offered full independent rear suspension. With well over 1000 Cortina based S7 kits supplied, the marque had entered a new era. 1994 had been a hell of a year, not least of which because it had inspired a more than rewarding change of direction.

The modern, thriving Robin Hood Engineering operation has unquestionably earned well its position as a leader in today's kit car industry. The point is, the company and its founder have never stood on their laurels and taken it easy. Constant evaluation and re-evaluation have taken place over the years, resulting in relentless development, regular improvements to models and hence an ever-improving deal for the customer. That's the important thing.

N.B. Although the following section of this chapter refers to Robin Hood Engineering's operations at its Sherwood factory, the company now does most of its kit car manufacturing at a new, much bigger premises in Mansfield Woodhouse, Notts. News of the move came too close to this book's press deadlines for all the necessary changes to be made, so we've left the following section unaltered as Robin Hood kit manufacturing processes are the same wherever they are carried out. In any case, the old Sherwood premises are still owned by the company and still serve various purposes essential to the car's existence.

The expansion to Mansfield Woodhouse was made in December 1994. The new factory uses 30,000 sq.ft. of space (compared to 10,000 sq.ft. at the old place) and, being entirely on one level (as opposed to three at Sherwood), is much more practical for the smooth running of a very busy production system. Possible maximum output is now around 100 kits per month, twice the previous level

Robin Hood Engineering Today

Since Richard Stewart hit on the idea of the Robin Hood and its derivatives, business at the company's works has really picked up. The main factory space in the old Wesleyan chapel at Sherwood is 9000 square feet and just next door there's a small trim shop of around 1000 square feet. A full time staff of 14 includes two laminators, two trimmers, two welders, two fabricators, two factory maintenance/delivery staff, one development engineer and one administrator.

"Everyone has a set job," says Richard Stewart. "If necessary, we can all help out when a certain department needs it." That seems to indicate that Robin Hood, although busy, has not adopted the strict production line approach. There's still a need for flexibility when it comes to production of the various kit options in a relatively small company.

RHE's workers are evenly spread out in various areas of the rambling, multi-level building. Because it's brick-built and forms a collection of several small and large rooms, the ancient Robin Hood works resembles the inside of a medieval castle. Some of the hidden alcoves look like they might have been the same back in the days of Friar Tuck. After years of use as a general garage business and for several different kinds of kit and rebodying projects, there's a lot of equipment and car parts everywhere. Some of the stacks of parts look like they haven't moved for some time.

Fronting Mansfield Street, at pavement level, there's the Robin Hood showroom where up to four demonstrators have often taken pride of place. These have ranged from standard four-cylinder cars with Cortina running gear right through to the V8 option with SD1 donor parts and the V12 test-bed, which

used Jaguar parts. Next door to the showroom is a small and very busy office from where the super-efficient receptionist, Gina, appears to co-ordinate the company's day-to-day schedule. She is also mastering the CNC plasma cutting machine from a small computer here. This must make Robin Hood one of the only kit car companies to boast female-operated CAD/CAM facilities in-house!

On the same level there's a large metal storage area with facilities for cutting, bending and otherwise shaping the sheet and tubular steel used in the construction of the kits. Massive old guillotines and presses cope with the tasks that make the Robin Hood monocoque possible. It's a wonderful collection of heavy equipment, rather like a line-up of siege engines waiting to be rolled into action as the need arises. Chassis made uniquely from tubular steel don't require anywhere as much machinery to get the raw materials prepared for final assembly.

Other hidden corridors and winding stairs take the visitor to different levels of the factory building where there's a small in-house laminating shop, parts storage areas, chassis assembly works and space for part-builds and kit collation. A large and cluttered exterior yard contains all kinds of motoring debris, the purpose of which is probably yet another secret

Simple Cortina front suspension was retained in its entirety for the S7, including the subframe.

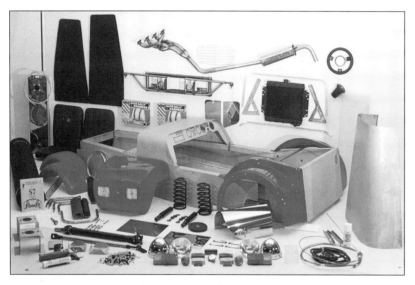

Top: The Sierra based monocoque with fibreglass wings and nose cone. Black plastic protects the stainless while in transit and during much of the build. Below: A Zintex monocoque with complete kit package for the Sierra Robin Hood.

tucked away in Richard Stewart's own random access memory. The works has been consistently improved when a gap in kit production allows but it still doesn't get anywhere near a 'tidy' rating.

Customers and potential customers won't have to delve too closely into the Robin Hood empire before discovering that things are slightly different there. Mr. Stewart certainly isn't a conformist, as the specification of the kits shows. One of the first house rules is that the company is closed to the public all week. Saturday is the visiting day for all comers, unless the staff are attending a show that weekend. Nothing is permitted to get in the way of the production schedule during the week.

Mr. Stewart, despite his shiningly avant-garde sense of humour, is every bit the pragmatist and the Robin Hood set-up reflects this. No efforts are wasted on fripperies or the trappings of success. Visitors

won't find suit-clad sales staff and a boss hidden away in a tenth floor penthouse suite. He is very much involved in the day-to-day running of the company at the nitty-gritty level and wears the correct stuff for the shop-floor.

Why doesn't the Robin Hood MD reserve his considerable inventive talent for continual research and development of the kits? After all, the S7 Zintex and stainless steel construction options really broke new ground in the kit car trade. "I'm not a designer or a stylist," remarks Mr. Stewart. "We've got a professional engineer for that sort of work. What I do is make cars."

There's little doubt, though, that Richard Stewart has been the inspiration behind much of the evolutionary development lavished on these kits. Over the last two years Robin Hood Engineering has settled down to produce an extended production run of the S7 and Sierra based kits. A long and continuous series of refinements, improvements and re-designs has culminated most notably in 1994's latest Sierra specification kit, and this is now the sole production model.

How important is Robin Hood Engineering in terms of its output size? Mr. Stewart was not totally forthcoming when asked exactly how many kits the company has produced to date. However, the name is now well known throughout the industry and there are strong indications that a good share of the market for this type of car currently goes to the Nottingham company. That doesn't necessarily put it in the Caterham/Westfield league quite yet but it could well be running in third or fourth place behind them in the production of home assembly kits for the UK market.

The Recent Model Range

It would be safe to bet that Robin Hood Engineering has only ever productionised a small proportion of Richard Stewart's many ideas. Unfortunately, the conservatism of the kit buying public is a severe limitation to the sort of car that a small manufacturer could reasonably hope to sell profitably. In very plain terms, this means that the UK kit buyer is a predictable creature – hence the large choice of kits which outwardly resemble the ever-popular Lotus and Caterham Sevens.

Robin Hood's S7 took over from the spaceframe S6 model in the late 'eighties. In fact, it was first shown in 1989 and the first orders were taken at the Stoneleigh kit car show of that year. In those days, it was a Dolomite-based kit using a tubular steel spaceframe chassis. The Triumph donor was raided for its front and rear suspension, instruments, loom and various other components, with Robin Hood supplying extra suspension parts for the job.

"We needed something that was quicker to assemble than a welded steel spaceframe," remembers RHE boss Stewart. "That's when I commissioned an engineer to computer-design the steel monocoque version produced from our stocks of stainless steel sheet." In 1990, therefore, the monocoque Dolomite based S7 appeared as an option to the spaceframe kit. (Monocoque is a word used to describe a structure formed as a stressed shell, made primarily from sheet or moulded materials, as opposed to a tubular chassis or frame).

This first experimental monocoque S7 project predominantly used 22-gauge lightweight sheet. The whole central body structure was both stiff and very light into the bargain. Subsequently, the earlier spaceframe version died a death and the lightweight monocoque version was produced until June 1991. After that, a new monocoque was designed, using thicker 16-gauge (1.6mm) stainless steel sheet and Cortina live axle donor parts.

Retaining the 'one donor' principle to which the company always tries to adhere, Mr. Stewart incorporated the Cortina front subframe and the entire rear axle configuration into the new S7 kit. As ever, there was room for improvement in the very mediocre standard Cortina suspension set-up. At the beginning of 1992, Robin Hood Engineering added a fifth rear suspension arm to better locate the axle against tramp or wind-up.

This fifth link didn't mean that the S7 had a proprietary five-link rear end. The latter is usually taken to be a live axle located by four radius rods or other types of suspension arm as well as a Panhard rod. The RHE fifth link was actually a small radius rod extending rearwards from the centre of the rear bulkhead to the top of the differential housing.

The builder had to drill a hole through the top of the axle casing and then file it conical so that the tapered ball-joint at the trailing end of the fifth link could be securely bolted through the axle casing. An adjustable, threaded end to the fifth link meant that the car's builder could then alter the angle of the differential nose so that it was parallel with the face of the engine/bell-housing mounting. Rather a clever way of reducing some of the Cortina axle's usual antics.

Up at the front end, the welded steel Cortina front subframe got a good trimming from the car's builder as various sections of it – the engine mounts, for instance – were no longer necessary. The first version, fitted to most Cortina-based kits up to the end of 1993, retained the standard wishbones, tie rods and shock absorbers etc. Unfortunately, the protruding front prongs of the subframe, which serve to locate the tie rods, could be easily seen protruding from the nose moulding and were usually hidden behind a set of after-market driving lamps.

In addition to a chassis for the standard Cortina front suspension, there was also a chassis specifically designed for fully independent front suspension with all-new parts. It made use of the Cortina front brakes, uprights and hubs but offered new adjustable wishbones mounted to chassis pick-up points. A few versions of this special front end came and went but by late 1993, it was standardised, using specially made coil-over shock absorbers. This system was made available on the S7 DeLuxe specification kit and was not a retro-fit item for other models.

In order to produce a budget version of the S7, sometimes called the Economy 7, a monocoque chassis was produced initially from mild steel sheet. This cost a lot less, even though it meant that the builder would have to finance a thorough paint job for the entire tub, inside and out, to prevent rust. The

Kits are despatched with everything slotted into the main tubs to make transit as easy as possible.

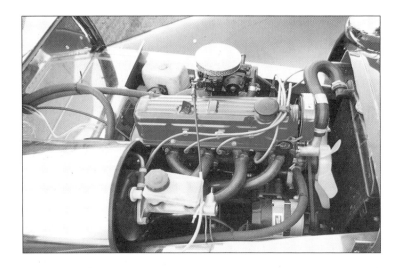

Top: Typical installation for most builders will be Ford's OHC Pinto engine in either 1600cc or 2-litre form. Above: This Cortina based Robin Hood has been fitted with the donor's dash pod fitted carefully behind the main dash panel.

mild steel option was soon replaced by Zintex coated steel for better rust prevention.

"Galvanised steel rejects paintwork but this Zintex is a really good base for paint." Richard Stewart's budget version, officially known as the 'S7 Part Assembled Body Kit with Zintex coated steel body/chassis unit', retailed at just £1568.63 including VAT at the end of 1993.

RHE's WB specification kits became standard for Cortina front suspension versions in late 1993. In order to avoid having that unsightly pair of front subframe mounts protruding either side of the lower part of the nosecone, the whole Cortina subframe was turned through 180 degrees, effectively facing rearwards. However, the wishbones and hub/uprights remained on their respective sides.

The noticeable difference was that the front tie

rods, having previously been semi-trailing links, became leading links, or compression struts. No more odd bits sticking out at the front of the car. Other specification changes included the switch from GRP to steel rear bodywork (although GRP rear wings were retained) and the factory fitment of the scuttle sections.

To add yet another version to the range seemed a little excessive but, nevertheless, the race for V8-powered vehicles caught up with Robin Hood Engineering as well. This evolutionary version was designed using many Rover SD1 donor parts, including the torque tube rear live axle and the V8 engine and gearbox all supplied by the builder. The company put together a very comprehensive package of parts for this beefed-up version, including Granada vented front discs, adjustable twin-wishbone front suspension and many other standard and special parts. Quite a few of them had been fitted to the kit at the factory.

It was dubbed the S8 but its 1993 price tag of £8225 inclusive of VAT meant that customers were few and far between and only about six examples were sold. At the end of the day, many builders were looking at a total budget of at least £10,000 for a nice home-built example. Cheap for ultimate performance but still a little extravagant for many buyers in a recession. "What some customers did was buy a standard Cortina-based kit and put a Rover V8 in that instead. They had to do the alterations themselves if they wanted to take that route."

Following the demise of the S7 name and its use of the Cortina as donor, today's sole production Robin Hood is the Sierra based model. Body/chassis unit prices still start remarkably cheaply – at £1195 plus VAT for the zinc-coated mild steel assembly – and the package is still remarkably comprehensive, including absolutely everything required bar the donor vehicle parts.

Most desirable of the various kit specifications available is the stainless steel Deluxe kit which currently sells for £1495 plus VAT. Big attraction is of course the sparkling finish of the structure manufactured from 1.6mm mirror-like stainless steel – along with the fact that a superb looking machine can be put on the road for a temptingly meagre £2000 or thereabouts. In the case of the zinc-coated mild steel monocoque version, this figure can be reduced to a truly measly £1500 or so.

So what's at the heart of the Robin Hood kits? What makes the monocoque construction so special? Basically, it is usually a method of manufacture reserved for the computerised mass-production car firms. The principles aren't particularly new and the Robin Hood's monocoque structure isn't particularly revolutionary in the light of other modern engineering achievements. The difference is that kit car manufacturers usually turn to GRP when they want to make a monocoque structure.

Having much experience with all types of car bodywork in the past, the staff of Robin Hood Engineering already had access to various meaningful tools which could cope with sheet steel. It seemed like a logical step to take when a huge stock of stainless steel sheet became available all of a sudden. Richard Stewart decided to make the most effective use of the materials he had – which were easier to work with and less costly than trying for a GRP monocoque. A lot lighter as well.

Having had a design engineer go through the process on computer, Richard then instituted a production system to cut the stainless sheet to the right sizes and then to trim, fold and weld the sub-assemblies into one central steel tub. The system could be much the same for stainless steel sheet as for Zintex steel sheet. With the appropriate experts employed in their respective departments, a pretty efficient production schedule was set up.

No more messing around with the rather meticulous and time-honoured process of cutting, jigging and welding up steel tubes of various sections and gauges. This was to be a different ball game altogether. The main structure of the Robin Hood kits is their central body tub. Folded and welded sections come together to produce a body/chassis with torsional strength in the front and rear bulkheads, the transmission tunnel and relatively large side sill sections. Beam stiffness also stems from the tunnel and side sills, the latter extending forwards towards the front suspension mounts.

Factory MIG and TIG welding bring the essential components together, leaving the builder to do very little in the way of structural body assembly. The more difficult shapes, the compound curves, are taken care of with GRP mouldings supplied in red, green or blue final gel coat colour. These parts are typically the rear bodywork and wings, front clamshell or cycle wings, nosecone etc. The vast majority of the car is steel, either Zintex or stainless.

One of the biggest difficulties with sheet steel structures is where to attach the high-stress

This is Which Kit? magazine's own Cortina based Robin Hood which was completed without any major trauma and certainly looked the part when finished.

Above: This may look just like any other Robin Hood, but it most definitely isn't. Below: Under the innocent looking bonnet lies a massive Jaguar V12 engine! They don't get much bigger.

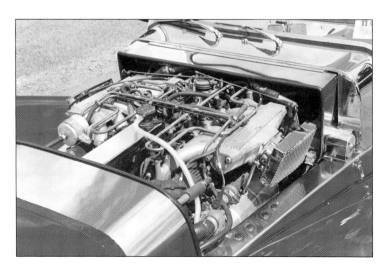

components. Such things as the mounting points for suspensions, seatbelts, roll-over bar, gearbox and engine mounts. It must not be forgotten that the Sierra itself is of sheet steel monocoque structure, so various components are already designed with attachment to a monocoque in mind.

An integral roll-over bar, braced rearwards, is an optional Robin Hood extra and is welded to the bodyshell. Seatbelt mounts can be supplied for three-point harnesses or for lap/diagonal belts and load-dissipating brackets and mounts are included for the suspension components. There are a few steel tubes in the construction of the body but these are kept to a minimum.

As the Sierra is the only donor for mechanical parts, it's no surprise to find that it is also the principal donor for engines/gearboxes as well. Namely the Pinto engines in 2-litre and 1.6-litre formats, with a four or five-speed 'box and a Ford or Weber downdraft carburettor. "I think the Kent engines are past it," claims Mr. Stewart. "The Toyota and Fiat twin-cams are the most common alternatives to the Pinto but the Rover V8 is probably the most powerful engine anyone has used in one of our cars up to now."

Robin Hood's Sierra-based, Sierra-powered demonstrator has been fitted with standard 2-litre Pinto engine. With an aftermarket air filter the builder can avoid having to put a bulge in the bonnet. Like various other Cortina/Sierra based cars of this style, the Robin Hood is a fairly big vehicle. It's quite a bit bigger than the Lotus Seven or the Caterham Super Seven and that does have the knock-on advantage of ample legroom and seat width. The literature claims room for drivers of 6'1". That certainly is the case. Standard trimmed bench seats have to be fitted specifically for the driver in question but builders have the option of fitting narrow reclining seats for shorter occupants. A simple and neat carpet and trim set gives a tidy standardised appearance to the Robin Hood.

It is a very easy vehicle to drive. Out on the open road, it soon establishes itself as a comfortable touring sportster and, with the Sierra independent rear suspension, it avoids much of the hard go-kart like traits of other live-axled cars. There's plenty of grip and traction and, with the Sierra's 5-speed 'box, progress can be as frenetic or relaxed as the driver chooses. At the front, in order to overcome the problem of the Sierra's strut assembly, Robin Hood has designed its own set-up with in-board coil-over dampers working on top rocker arm wishbones. It leaves a clean and uncluttered front suspension that also seems to work well.

Perhaps the Sierra donor makes the Robin Hood product a far more forgiving road car? It can very easily deal with rough road surfaces due to the compliant suspension. Ford's Pinto engine is ever eager but still rather a slouch compared to a twin-cam or a well-balanced version of the same unit.

Superb servo-assisted braking, smooth steering feel and manageable pedals all contribute towards making this a superb introduction to small-ish sports car driving. The Sierra base means that the spares are generally as cheap as you can buy for any car and Robin Hood's own parts pricelist is very competitive. The company offers customers a very competitively priced and comprehensive set of new parts for refurbishing much of the Ford running gear.

Probably the biggest attraction of the Robin Hood kits has been the sheer brilliance of the stainless steel finish of the central bodywork and bonnet. Most owners elect to keep the bodyshell in its polished state, with the only concessions to colour being the gel-coated wings and rear bodywork. It's an impressive effect out on the road, especially when the sun is shining down. It's also much more durable than alloy sheet, which is easily scratched and dented and becomes irresistibly dull with age and oxidation.

It is interesting to see just how much new ground has been broken by Robin Hood's monocoque in its first few years of production. With comfortable sales figures, and a good research budget, there's no telling just what changes will be made to the kit over the next few years. It's unlikely that things will ever be left just as they are at Robin Hood Engineering and the potential for a super-strong, super-lightweight monocoque car requiring minimal material input and minimal build effort is surely within reach. It's just a question of how hard they can work their resident engineer.

The Future

The fortunes of Robin Hood Engineering over the next few years are going to be generated, not surprisingly, by the need to make economically viable the large new factory at Mansfield Woodhouse. 30,000 sq.ft. is

Here you can clearly see the Sierra based Robin Hood's neat front suspension with inboard coil-overs and rocker top wishbones.

quite a lot of space to make fully cost-effective with kit car manufacturing alone. Yet the current Sierra based Robin Hood is already a volume-made product and a fully proven one, too. In kit car industry terms, regular output of 12-15 units per week is truly 'mass' production.

The engineering machinery, manufacturing systems, skills, parts and materials supplies and detailed costings are already in place to make good use of the new factory, but to date virtually every Robin Hood kit made has gone to a British customer. What about business expansion via exports, for instance?

"We certainly plan to investigate export markets soon," says Richard Stewart. "I see it happening via relationships and partnerships with people or companies abroad, a sort of franchising arrangement maybe. For example, we are currently dealing with a strong enquiry from Taiwan. A company there seems quite serious about an initial twenty turn-key cars provided the first example successfully passes their

The Sierra based Robin Hood has attracted an impressive number of sales for the company, largely due to it's incredibly comprehensive yet competitive price.

environmental and construction tests. But I would naturally worry that they'd simply copy car number one and get on with making it themselves, so that's where the franchising comes in."

On the subject of possible fresh new models, what would Robin Hood produce if the research budget was no barrier? Apart from the original S7 and its many derivatives, nothing entirely different has been produced since the early days of Ferrari Daytona replicas.

"I'm not a designer," Richard reminds us. "We've had an awful lot of drawings and renderings sent here by various enthusiastic car stylists keen to see an advanced or futuristic interpretation of the sevenesque theme on a Robin Hood chassis. But I'm not sure the public want that sort of car. It's the traditional roadster style they like, particularly the older enthusiasts.

"We did invest lots of money in a battery driven child's car and I've given thought to something along robust off-road vehicle lines. I've made plenty of cars and anything in the way of a truly original shape is a long, long shot – even if you're using professional designers. Cheap sports cars always create consistent demand." Another reference to the conservatism of the British market for cars.

So far, the racing scene hasn't attracted the attention of the Robin Hood factory. "Some customers have said that they are preparing their cars for the circuit or for hillclimb events but I haven't heard anything yet." Mr Stewart has toyed with the idea of producing a lightweight racing monocoque from alloy but there seems to be little point in it. "The racing events are quite well covered by other specialist manufacturers."

With so many Robin Hood orders coming from the southern half of the country, Richard has also considered establishing, under his own supervision, a southern area offshoot of his company. But for the time being it looks like the time-consuming tasks of keeping up with kit demand and establishing fully the new factory will be an effective delay to any further expansion.

Since the inception of its early kits, Robin Hood Engineering has hit the big time in terms of kit car manufacturing success. The kit buying public might be a touch traditional in terms of the style of car it prefers but the existence of a stainless steel monocoque certainly hasn't been a disincentive to new customers, even if it has been a genuine departure from the norm. It's certainly been a refreshing new approach to amateur car building and no doubt that situation will continue at Robin Hood for a long time to come.

Top: With cycle style front wings, the Robin Hood looks quite different to the more conventional clamshell design. Above: The Sierra based Robin Hood looks set to ensure the company's ongoing good fortunes.

Chapter 7

Dax Rush

A Brief History

Anyone who has followed the kit car scene will be familiar with the DJ Sportscars company and its DAX kits. Although the Rush and Rush IRS are relatively

Brian and Pam Johns, DJ Sportscars' directors, stand in the company's smart showroom. You can see the company's other models, the Dax Tojeiro and Dax 40, in the background.

recent additions to the range, the DJ story goes back a long way.

As early as the 'sixties, Derek Johns ran a GRP laminating company which produced commercial and industrial mouldings from premises in Waltham Cross. He also manufactured a selection of replacement body panels for sports cars and made after-market styling packages for retail companies such as Ripspeed.

Things got pretty busy as car owners were less restoration-minded in those days. GRP panels and styling add-ons were being used on all manner of vehicles and the commercial side supplied mouldings for Plaxtons coaches, Norwest Holst Construction, British Airways and British Rail – to drop but a few names.

One of Derek's employees eventually came to run the business. This chap's name was Brian Johns, Derek's brother, and he and his wife, Pam, took over the laminating business. Unfortunately, cheaper imported steel panels from Taiwan and other far east sources started to make the replacement GRP body panels seem a trifle expensive by comparison.

Even experimentation with spray application of chopped strand mat and resin could not make the labour intensive laminating process competitive with these cheap imports. After a while, demand for the automotive mouldings dropped away and the company went on concentrating on the industrial work.

At the end of the seventies, a German entrepreneur arrived on the scene with an alloy 427 Cobra bodyshell. "Make moulds from this and produce GRP Cobra bodies for me," he instructed. It wasn't a particularly difficult job for Brian and Pam's company, as the staff regularly handled much more challenging tasks.

"The aluminium bodyshell was nowhere near true or symmetrical,"

remembers Brian. "We had to do a lot of improvement work to get it up to scratch. There wasn't even a floorpan or an inner body moulding, just the outer shell." When the delighted German dealer came along with his trailer to collect the mouldings, he would load up as many complete bodies as he could and then find room for the remaining body mouldings by cutting them into quarters and lashing the whole lot to the trailer.

Kit builders had it tough in those days. The German method was to attach these Cobra-like shells to the ladder chassis and running gear of imported Corvettes. Just like a rebodying exercise but perhaps a bit more complex than that...

Demand from Germany had dried up for a couple of years when DJ Sportscars moved to its current premises at Edinburgh Place in Harlow, Essex, in 1982. The DJ management got together and decided that there might be a little business in the UK on the Cobra

Above and below: An original Jurgen Mohr Rush in full racing spec. With over 300bhp on tap from a highly tuned Cosworth turbo engine it was viciously quick. Vents in the nose cone duct air to the intercooler (which you can see below just in front of the engine).

Above: Stripped out interior of German racer backs up the feeling that this is one very serious car indeed. Note the instantly accessible screw-in fuses on the right of the dashboard. Below: Subtlety has never been a Rush strong point.

lookalike shell side, so they put a small ad in the *Exchange & Mart* for the basic outer shell in GRP.

They were right. There was quite a healthy demand for the very basic offering and buyers (seemingly impulse buyers to a large extent) flocked to DJ to pick up the shells. Aluminium bodies were available elsewhere but were, as ever, incredibly expensive. The ever-inventive British sports car enthusiasts were using the DJ GRP shells to make Cobra lookalikes based on Reliant Scimitar, Triumph and even home-made chassis. 30-40 of the DJ shells were sold in pretty short order.

This was the basis of today's successful Dax 427 Cobra lookalike business. It's probably been the best-selling Cobra kit in the UK, since the company was one of the first to go ahead and design a full body/chassis package for the amateur builder. For several years they've even enjoyed the official support of John Tojeiro, the

designer of the AC Ace, which was the forerunner of the AC Cobra range. That, however, is a story for another book...

Along the way, Brian and Pam Johns have taken on various other kinds of kit car projects. One of their earlier deviations from the Cobra theme was an invention of their works foreman, Gary Sanders. Gary designed and constructed an off-road rail called the Nevada and instantly proved it as a winner on the AWDC circuits. Lots of beefy after-market parts, all vaguely related to VW mechanicals, turned the 'cage' chassis into an airborne flier.

Around 1983, they took on a little known creation called the Charger, which lasted a couple of years before it was sold on. In 1984, they first started experimenting with the VW-based Porsche Speedster lookalikes in standard and in Californian trim. They still supply these kits today but they're not a best-seller by any means compared to the Tojeiro.

Towards 1987/8, DJ entered into a joint project with Ken Attwell of KVA to improve and supply the kit-form Dax/KVA 40, a Ford GT40 lookalike. After some prolonged research effort, nothing came of the project and Dax went their own way in developing a completely new 40, now called simply the Dax 40.

Throughout this period of experimentation, the Cobra kit, now called the Dax Tojeiro, was consistently improved and modified. It had new chassis options, new body options and even some racing success at the hands of Martin Harrison in 1988. It was, and still is, a remarkably popular kit style, eclipsing all other attempts by DJ to branch out. The addition of ex-Ford specialist Peter Walker to the DJ team helped to speed along the introduction of the beautiful Supertube version of the Dax Tojeiro chassis.

Things changed in early 1990. A German fellow by the name of Jurgen Mohr, who was also the German agent for Dax Tojeiro kits and parts, mentioned his own Rush kit to the management at DJ. This was a self-assembly vehicle which he had apparently been producing for a number of years, for European customers, and it looked very much like a butch and modernised version of the Lotus Seven.

Knowing the perennial popularity of such speedy roadsters in the UK market, DJ was interested in striking up a deal in order to become the sole UK agent for the Mohr Rush kits, which would continue to be produced in Germany and sold in the UK as the Dax Rush. Adverts were published, deposits came in and the German demonstrator cars, in all their incredibly lurid livery, became real attention-grabbers

Following trouble with the German chassis, DJ set about designing its own improved version. Here you can see another Rush chassis in mid-construction on the chassis jig.

in magazines and at shows.

It wasn't as simple as that, though. It transpired that the Rush chassis was on the wrong side of copyright laws as it was far too close to the Westfield product. This meant that the only way DJ could market the car here was to redesign it. This they duly did, with customers patiently waiting in the wings.

Gary Sanders and Peter Walker set about making a complete new chassis for the first live-axled version and then for the evolutionary IRS model. New GRP and alloy bodywork was also styled and produced. All in all, the end product received a very intense bout of refinement work.

It had already become obvious that new customer response to the Rush was favourable. Here was a kit which could rival the Tojeiro for popularity. The first all-Dax demo Rush appeared around August 1991.

DJ Sportscars Today

DJ Sportscars International Ltd. is now the grand title of Brian and Pam Johns' business empire and their British built kits have been sent all around the world. The 9200 sq. ft. Edinburgh Place works in Harlow is now mostly given over to kit car production and the large, graphic lettering along the front wall is an ample landmark to confirm your arrival.

The customer entrance doors open out into a small lobby where there's a tiny reception to your right. Dead ahead you'll see the showroom area with a selection of Tojeiro and Rush models and usually

The first Dax Rush demonstrator featured a wild semi fluorescent paint scheme. Massive rear wheelarches (housing the Cortina live axle) and square headlamps have almost become a Rush trademark. The car ran a mildly tuned 2-litre Pinto engine with twin Dell'Orto carburettors and 4-speed gearbox.

DJ's first demonstrator was very simply trimmed but looked none the worse for it. Seats in this early car came from one of the company's other models, the awesome Dax 40 (GT 40 replica). Above left: Simple double wishbone front suspension works very well and is mated to Cortina front uprights and brakes. Motorcycle indicator and square headlamp are neat styling touches.

One of the first customer built Rush's was this TR7 engined example. The car looked quite different when painted in only one colour! Aluminium bonnet allowed for the tiny louvres you can just see.

one or several groups of enthusiasts getting the tour. Brian and Pam's son Simon has also come into the DJ stable and there's an evens chance of meeting any of the Johns here.

A corridor off to your right leads to the several busy offices where a good standard of administrative efficiency is maintained. With orders for all manner of components coming in from around the world, there's a never-ending stream of mail and telephone enquiries. Plenty of evidence here to show that DJ is bigger than an average kit car concern, as various staff members can always be seen circulating around the building.

Carry on to the end of this corridor and one of the doors lets you into the nitty gritty side of the works. This is the design and fabrication shop combined. Here you'll find the large jigs for the Rush and Rush IRS, as well as for the standard Tojeiro chassis. There's plenty of stock steel, various engines and lots of welding/cutting equipment.

A large roller-shutter door opens out onto the yard behind the works. Not such a neat area this,

Very early on DJ was designing an independent rear suspension version of the Rush. K300 DAX was the first IRS demonstrator. The 300 hinted at the output of the highly tuned Cosworth turbo engine under the bonnet. Below: A completed chassis with independent rear suspension. In the background you can see a Dax 40 chassis.

but every company must have a cupboard for its skeletons. Dotted around the yard are chassis ready to go out and other bits of bodywork belonging to forgotten projects. Piles of donor parts can also be found there, as DJ is often asked to supply its customers with reconditioned mechanical components – especially the Jaguar running gear for the Cobra replicas.

On the far left, there's more room for prototype development. At the time of our visit, we saw that a Rush chassis was indeed the basis for a new model or version. We'll say a little more about that one in the final part of this chapter. Suffice to say that DJ doesn't rest on its laurels for very long.

Below: Cosworth turbo installation is extremely well executed thanks to minor modifications supplied by Dax. Bottom: Neat new dash design is a welcome departure from more conventional plank-like offerings. Sierra column stalks are also a big improvement.

Another doorway and another left-wards move will take you towards the very big laminating area. Depending upon the state of orders that week, the area can be full of moulds for Tojeiros, industrial equipment or even for truck cabs etc. They look huge when seen inside a building. Several laminating staff are always to be seen preparing GRP here. Remember that the laminating side was the making of this particular company.

To the left of the GRP workshop, a fairly generous bay has been created for kit assembly and partial builds to customer specification. A typical sight is several Rush IRS chassis, in various colours, set up on trestles side by side for preparation work prior to delivery. All manner of part-completed vehicles are to be found here throughout the year. Many of the Tojeiro and Dax 40 orders specify a certain degree of kit preparation so a rolling chassis build is not uncommon.

Another door adjacent to this assembly area brings us back into the showroom, opposite the customer entrance. Only one Rush was available for viewing at that time but it was no ordinary car. This was the latest IRS version of the marque, again developed wholly by DJ staff, and it has been fitted with a turbo-charged Ford Sierra Cosworth engine and box. Added to that are some extra tuning goodies to up the horsepower. This is, obviously, a very quick and powerful car. DJ claims 310bhp potential for this one, depending upon the boost setting selected.

Another large roller-shutter door lets daylight stream into the showroom and is evidence of a very active test-driving policy. There's a pretty permanent stream of Tojeiro and Rush traffic in and out of the display area as keen enthusiasts (and quite often their spouses) are taken for breathtaking sprints around the Essex hinterland by one of DJ's people.

It is more likely that only very sincere customers will be given the controls of the powerful demo cars. A customer once stuffed one of the big-block V8-powered Tojeiros into a tree only a few yards out of the showroom door. His shiny production sports car, a legend in its own right, had been no preparation for real power-to-weight ratio!

Those who work with the extremely quick Daxs all the time have adopted a quiet tolerance of the driving experience that enthusiasts may have gained from mere production cars. It must be amusing to see the effects of a *truly* fast car on someone who might

have been lulled into a false sense of security by owning what is only *reputed* to be a fast car.

"It's good to be producing a selection of completely different cars," says Brian. "It makes things a lot more interesting when there are plenty of different jobs to be done." With the Tojeiro and the Rush selling at about the same rate, along with the options in each model range, there's quite a large set of variations. Brian estimates that around 140 Rush kits have been sold so far, while the model quite obviously has a great future ahead of it.

One of the first independent rear suspension Rush's to be completed by a customer was Chris Cocklin's Ford 2.8-litre V6 powered example. Despite this unit's added weight, the car performed extremely well, with the injection engine providing smooth, fuss-free power.

Current Models

What with the copyright debacle and disappointment with the number of design shortcomings in the original imported kit, DJ took the difficult route and basically re-invented the Rush. The company's original live-axled Rush demo car, painted in the same wildly graphic patterns as the early German cars, hit the streets in 1991.

Perhaps the biggest visual difference, apart from the very un-British colour scheme, was the sheer width of the car. It wasn't the first small two-seater to use a Cortina-width live axle but those massively wide rear wheels and tyres gave the ensemble another few inches, exaggerating the low and wide stance of the car. In particular, the big expanses of rear bodywork and rear wheel arches proved to be impressive attention-grabbers.

What goes into a live-axled Rush? Starting from the rear end, you'll find the Cortina live axle which is always professionally modified at the DJ works. The customer, if supplying the donor parts for the build-up, must present the cleaned and dismantled axle at the Dax works for the appropriate brackets to be welded in place and must then reassemble the axle components. Obviously, the axle then has to go back to DJ if they are to fit it to the chassis on the customer's behalf.

DJ's interpretation of the live axle location for the Rush involves twin (trailing) radius rods each side of the axle and a Panhard rod. This is a classic five-link rear axle set-up in the time-honoured fashion, which does a good job of eradicating undesirable lateral axle

Experienced racing driver, Martin Harrison, won the 1992 750 Motor Club Phoenix Kit Car Challenge when he campaigned this hairy Rover V8 powered, IRS Dax Rush. He won no less than ten of the season's events! Here's the car being campaigned by new owner, Hugh Law.

movement and rear end steer. Adjustable coil-over shock absorbers replace the Cortina springs and shocks but the standard rear drum brakes are retained.

A shortened, remanufactured propshaft is required and this attaches the differential flange to whichever gearbox the customer intends to use. It's no surprise that most Rush customers opt for the user-friendly 2-litre Pinto SOHC four, despite the weight penalties of its all-iron construction. It can use various standard four or five-speed gearboxes from the Ford range.

"There's very little interest in the Ford X-flow engines," affirms Brian Johns. "Customers have asked us to fit various different units. There's the Cologne V6, Rover V8, Astra GTE twin-cam and the Cosworth twin-cam." Customers for the beefier engines will, however, be guided towards the IRS Rush as its rear end is more resilient than the Cortina equipment on the live-axled car.

Up front, the live-axled Rush shares its specification with the IRS version as the Cortina donor (always Mk.4 or 5) supplies the brake calipers, discs, hub/uprights and the track rods. A Mk.2 Escort supplies the inner and outer steering column and the steering rack centre section. DJ Sportscars supplies the unequal length upper and lower wishbones, coil-over shock absorbers, special track rod ends, special upper and lower ball-joints, a lower steering column extension and various shims, mounts and, of course, a full brake pipe kit.

It's obvious that a substantial amount of thought

has gone into the preparation of a purpose-built front suspension assembly which suits the car best. A wide range of front and rear suspension setting adjustments means that amateur builders, with factory guidance, can configure their cars to cope better with different wheels, tyres, engines, gearboxes and driving conditions.

In terms of its structure, the Rush follows the lessons taught by Colin Chapman and other race winners of the past. Keep it light, keep it small gauge and keep it as stiff as possible. In fact, most cars currently aspiring to a Seven-esque role are a fair bit more substantial than Chapman would have permitted. People are asking for more horsepower and torque so manufacturers have to be sure of their chassis.

Mild steel square section tubes form the Rush chassis. The builder or the factory will add the alloy panels for the floor, bulkheads and scuttle top but these are not designed to be structural sheets. Most of the chassis' stiffness is inherent in the triangulated perimeter sections, the front and rear bulkheads and the well-triangulated front suspension mounting section. Nothing new or revolutionary here.

Although the wheel track front and rear gives a very wide appearance to the Rush, this doesn't mean that there is an exceptional quantity of interior space on board. The cockpit area isn't notably wide and is only sufficient for drivers of realistic adult dimensions.

Latest incarnation of the Rush is the high-tech Quadra 4x4. Could this be the ultimate sevenesque roadster? Here you can see the first ever car, built specially for a customer, alongside the two-wheel-drive Cosworth demonstrator.

Six feet tall isn't a problem in the Rush and shorter drivers are accommodated by adding another seat-back cushion. The seats are basic squabs and as such are unadjustable.

All of the outer body panels and mudguards are supplied in GRP and can be self-coloured or supplied with a basic finish for final paintwork. There's also the extra cost option of alloy panels for the bonnet and for the main body sides. You don't have to go for 10" wide rear rims as the rear mudguards can be supplied in a variety of widths to suit the rim that you prefer – or the ones that you can afford!

If you opt for the IRS rear end, the chassis supplied will use the same front suspension as the live-axled Rush but the back end will have been quite considerably altered. The main reason for this is, of course, that the frame needs to support a Ford Granada Mk.3 (Scorpio shape) differential or the equivalent item from a Sierra 4x4 – NOT the standard Sierra differential more often used in these circumstances.

The builder needs to find a Scorpio differential,

full-width half-shafts, rear discs, calipers and handbrake mechanism. None of the Ford axle locating machinery is retained as DJ supplies the wide-based, square section tubular wishbones and cast alloy uprights all tailor-made for the job.

There's a supplement at the end of the Rush build manual, which is mostly dedicated to the live-axle and 'common' Rush components, that covers the assembly of the IRS rear end. Because there is a good deal of sophistication about an adjustable rear suspension, the manual goes into some detail as to how initial adjustments can be made for the rear toe-in, camber etc.

It's interesting to note that the Ford rear brake calipers are swapped from left to right for the Rush, to allow for correct handbrake operation and other assembly procedures. This means that the bleed nipples end up at the bottom of the calipers, which must be unbolted and upended for successful brake bleeding. On the subject of braking, very impressive is DJ's system of converting the solid disc Cortina front brake assembly to a more efficient system which is compatible with the five-stud rear wheel fitment of the IRS Rush.

Gary Sanders, responsible for much of the Rush development work, has established how certain elements of the Cortina and Granada wheel bearing packages can be interchanged so that the Cortina front uprights can be used with the Granada hubs and vented front discs. Add to this a factory modification for the uprights and the Granada calipers can also be fitted.

Can you see it? If you weren't concentrating, the front driveshafts of the Quadra 4x4 could easily be missed. A complete new front suspension system had to be designed to accommodate the extra driveshafts. The more conventional set-up can be seen on the right.

Top braking efficiency is offered via a bias adjustable twin-circuit, twin master cylinder hydraulic system. Up to the middle of 1993, a Tilton pedal box was the requisite part but DJ has developed a specially made alternative.

A visit to DJ when the Cosworth-powered IRS Rush first hit the road saw the opportunity to talk shop with Mr. Sanders and to drive through the Essex countryside. While the car sat gleaming in the showroom, looking very understated in a deep metallic burgundy, he pointed out some of the alterations necessary for fitment of the Cosworth power unit. Because the Rush doesn't offer anything special in terms of engine bay width, the amount of peripheral accessories on the Cosworth Sierra mill has caused some design headaches. A few chassis rail modifications were necessary and the eventual fitment was a lot neater than the original attempt from Germany. That had the turbo charger protruding incongruously outside the engine compartment.

Even though the demonstrator car had a specially prepared engine, featuring adjustable boost pressure, many of the modifications would be required for any Cosworth Sierra fitment. A generous quantity of large and small pipes comes with the engine to help with the intercooler, the forced induction and the exhaust. Factory-completed modifications included some cutting and shutting of Ford steel and alloy components and repositioning of other parts. Most of this is in the interests of saving space width-wise.

Because particular attention had been paid to the new engine fitment, the Rush appeared to be a very refined product. No incongruous bonnet bulge, a subtle body blister on the nearside, trendy little speedboat-type chrome engine bay vents, three subtle vent grilles above the super-hot turbocharger, a well-concealed intercooler air intake duct inside the top of the nosecone and, of course, the mandatory sidepipe. When the bonnet is open, though, there isn't much spare space left behind. Thank goodness that it's a low-maintenance engine.

Externally and internally, it seemed indistinguishable from any other Rush, apart from the relatively conservative paint job. Removal of the spare driver's cushion allowed for good footwell length, for a 6' 1" driver in this case, and footwell width at the pedals was good enough for size ten feet. Although the screen height was generous, meaning that we weren't trying to look above and below the screen frame top, the single roll hoop was

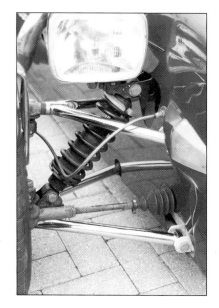

woefully low and would not have accomplished its designated task.

The car had a fairly conventional instrument and control layout, with the handbrake lever tucked away under the dashboard and the main instruments to the left of the dash centre, not in line-of-sight. No quirks in this department and very good functionality for furious and split-second driving. The interesting bit is the manual adjustment for maximum boost pressure limits, positioned neatly out of the way by the steering column...

If the standard Cosworth Sierra is rated by many mainstream writers as a true flier, then the Cosworth Rush is obviously all that and more. DJ claims 3.7 seconds to 60mph. We found that even with wettish roads, it was a genuinely capable car with massive performance pretensions – if you can forgive the abrupt personality of the turbocharged engine.

Because a vehicle such as the Rush is so light compared to the turbo unit's donor, there's an even better kick up the backside when the forced induction comes on line somewhere between 3000 and 4000 rpm. Obviously, nothing much happens before that deadline, with the Rush remaining rather docile. This leads to a tendency to drive with the foot to the floor as the 'hit' becomes really addictive.

In some ways, it's like having another set of cylinders which comes to life at 4000 rpm. This naturally leaves you very dissatisfied with anything that happens before that... Not for the faint-hearted, it's a vehicle which demands full concentration from the driver.

Unfortunately, the extra-wide Granada track, with wide wheels added, is a disadvantage around the country lanes. The Rush inevitably occupies more than half the road and this makes you a bit wary about any vehicles which might be coming the other way! It's a relatively big car compared to others of the genre which use the Escort or Marina rear axle.

Keeping the rev counter needle at 4000 or above, in order to avoid the turbo lag, is an exhilarating task. Lightning quick gearshifts via the tiny gear lever and minimal clutch pedal movement must happen like second nature. The rest of your concentration is devoted to seeing what's ahead and looking for blue lights behind. A genuine temptation to misbehave, this.

On a more practical note, the IRS system used by DJ is no exception to the general rule. It provides much better smoothness than a live axle, with less suspension fuss and good grip and traction

Above: This neat hinging nose cone isn't a standard option but its advantages in terms of access can instantly be appreciated. The turbo's intercooler is positioned just above and behind the standard radiator.

characteristics. This is particularly useful when cornering fast on a choppy surface. The worse the road surface, the more useful the IRS becomes. That's why so many live-axled cars are still capable performers in the kit car racing, where surfaces are usually ideally smooth.

No anomalies were found in the handling, steering or braking departments. Perhaps a slightly heavier castor angle would have improved self-centering up front and might have endowed the steering with a touch more road feel. That blower calms down the exhaust note nicely but the curious whines, coughs and other intake/exhaust gasping noises from the assorted turbo ancillaries create an odd cacophony to say the least.

In terms of overall quality, the Rush kit appears to be very good. Indeed, a standard Pinto engine fitment would make the assembly task a lot easier as the engine bay width, which has been found in an attempt to house the turbo parts with minimal modification, should cope nicely with simpler units.

DJ's interpretation of the Rush chassis is a stiff structure which thrives on the big bhp applications, seeming to crave more power. There's already a V8 option for the IRS Rush, using the Rover power plant, so that should take care of the power-hungry who don't like to use masses of rpm to get where they want to go.

Criticisms? Modifications to the Cosworth

ancillaries will increase the cost of the build or will exaggerate its complexity. A pronounced lag from the 'charger, with the eventual pick-up exaggerated by light vehicle weight, can become tiresome after a while. Fast driving is not effortless. The width of the vehicle will slow you down when you're not sure of the road ahead or when trying to overtake on minor roads. Narrower wheel/tyre/arch combinations and a torquey engine would cure just about all of these.

Given perfect conditions – dry weather, smooth, hot roads etc. – the massive grip and traction on offer combine with pin-point handling accuracy to make the Rush an extremely quick car with huge limits of adhesion. Surprisingly, it's still pretty predictable in the wet, even with large areas of rubber. Maximum rear wheel size is quoted as 10 x 15 with 255/50 VR 15 tyres. Up front, DJ recommends 8 x 15s with 205/50 x 15 tyres. Big bucks.

Just to smooth away any doubts, the *chosen* Rush race driver, Martin Harrison, took the first ever IRS Dax Rush to an all-conquering win in nearly every race in the 1992 750MC Phoenix Kit Car Challenge. Using a Rover V8 power plant, the new Rush managed to see off similarly-powered opposition which had benefitted from several seasons of track experience and expert preparation. Not a bad start, that.

What does it all cost? *Which Kit?* magazine estimated that the cost of a standard home-built IRS Cosworth Rush would probably come in at just under £9000 inclusive (March 1993 issue). That would be a high specification kit. In mid-1995, the basic kit for the live-axled Dax Rush cost £1395 +VAT and the (higher specification) IRS Rush kit cost £1895 +VAT. Because of DJ's relatively large size, their established supply lines and production facilities, there's a good range of optional equipment for the Rush. Most of the parts are available either off-the-shelf or at very short notice.

The Future

DJ reports that Rush sales are running about neck and neck with those of the Tojeiro. Around 90 Rush kits had gone out of the factory gates by mid 1993 and currently 50% of them tend to be the IRS version. What kind of development and research investment will these sales figures permit?

Dax Rush Quadra 4x4 (in the foreground) is powered by a mildly tuned 250bhp Cosworth turbo engine. Power output of conventional car (in the background) has recently been increased to nearer 350bhp. Quite a pair!

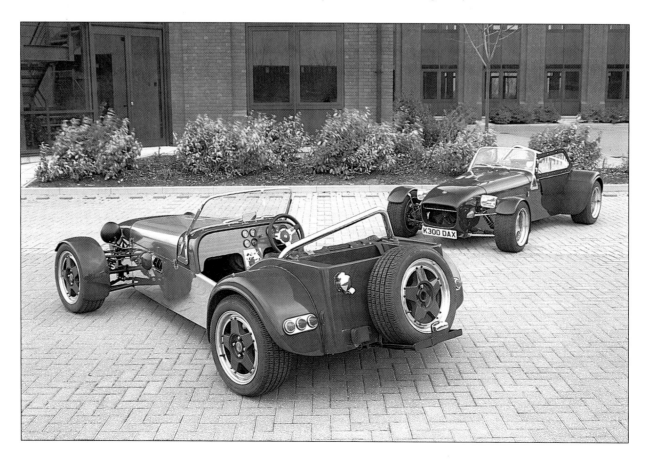

"The Rush is well down the road towards development of a 4x4 version," asserted DJ boss Brian Johns in 1993. By mid 1994 *Which Kit?* magazine had the opportunity of briefly testing the first completed Dax Rush 4x4 which is now marketed as the Rush Quadra 4x4. Initial driving impressions have been extremely promising while visually the Quadra is almost indistinguishable from its more conventional stablemates. Could this be the ultimate in seven-esque development? The 4x4 Quadra kit starts at £2195 +VAT.

What about Low Volume Type Approval for the Rush? "It's becoming very easy to get hold of good, cheap performance and sports cars these days," says Brian Johns. This hints at the genuine cost of getting a kit car through LVTA. It's far more than the £20-£30,000 often quoted as the rock bottom price. A lot of the expense comes in terms of time spent on research and on interpreting official regulations and specifications. Estimates of up to £250,000 and beyond are regularly quoted by those who have looked into the subject seriously.

Kit-form sales of the Rush are healthy enough, especially when one considers the poor state of the economy. The time does not seem right for any company to invest the kind of money needed for LVTA just yet. Even though there are very few production cars in the style of the Rush et al, you can still get a lot of thrill value on the second hand market for a relatively small quantity of money.

Martin Harrison continued to show that the Rush IRS is a winner in 1993. There are various other Rush models being prepared for racing in the 750MC Dax-Laser Challenge and for the bigger budget Newey Jewellers Super Sports Challenge. They will surely make a strong impression when they eventually arrive on the scene. "We've gained a good deal of credibility from our racing successes," claims Mr. Johns. That's probably true as there are examples of various other Seven clones out there on the race track most seasons – and an ever-increasing amount each year. Things are really hotting up.

In its own way, the Rush has brought a new and modern look to the scene. A move away from the narrow track and narrow tyres of yesterday and an affirmation of the macho width and aggression of today. Even if this isn't all in the best interests of roadgoing functionality, it means the car has become a real head-turner.

With one of the wild graphic paint jobs for which the Rush originally became notorious, you couldn't really be accused of trying to recapture the personality of someone else's traditional car... As far as the customer is concerned, a visit to the DJ works will confirm that this is one of the biggest and busiest companies in the industry. The early success of the Rush shows that they have been building cars for years before they took this project on.

A decent construction manual, good spares supply and services, technical advice down the phone and a progressive approach to customer relations have always been a recipe for success at DJ. The Rush has been treated to all of these benefits from day one, jumping the queue in a sense. It will be a big seller in the future.

Chapter 8

Vindicator Sprint

A Brief History

Engineering, racing, tea and sandwiches. That's a wide-ranging CV in anyone's language. Especially when it all ends up in kit car manufacture. Vindicator boss Roger Lea started off working for the family engineering firm, Arnold Lea and Son, near Halesowen. Their mainstay business was forging and casting for medium and heavy industrial customers and for agriculture. This is where he got a thorough and broad-based grounding in many aspects of metal work.

"I was involved with everything from making tea to cost accounting, tool design and manufacture and also some design drawing." Mr. Lea junior was to stay

Roger Lea's first foray into racing was in this Lotus 11 in 1963. Sadly, oil pressure problems forced him to retire fairly early on in the race.

in the family business for some years, eventually taking it over from his father.

Back in 1959, when he was seventeen, he first ventured into the wide world of car design. A Morris 8 was his raw material in this instance. When he had finished with the alloy re-panelling, it was renamed the Tripound! "It was a bit oversprung on its standard suspension." However, the car became a roadworthy machine and achieved its goals until replaced by an MGB. That was the start.

With his income from engineering work, Roger got hold of a Lotus 11 in 1963, to experiment with track racing. The project really didn't meet with the approval of his father, who thought that money and effort devoted to causes other than the family business were a bit of a waste. Mr. Lea senior wasn't too upset when young Roger had to retire early on the 11's first race (1000cc class), due to loss of oil pressure.

Undeterred, our racing convert decided that

Monoposto was the class to go for – and that meant he needed a proper single-seater racing car. More expense but there seemed to be little problem justifying it to himself. A phone call to a company called Progress Chassis revealed, not very helpfully, that chassis made to their drawings were "very expensive." The gent on the other end of the line mentioned in passing that Brabham might have a spare chassis going cheap.

Having then contacted Jack Brabham in Surrey, Roger was told that a prototype BT15 F3 frame, with quite a few additional parts, would be available for the princely sum of £55 the lot! Not a bad deal. Unfortunately, advice was taken from a racing acquaintance, a self-proclaimed car expert, who then proceeded to wreck the car's winning potential by mortally rearranging the suspension pick-up points etc. Oh well.

Anyway, the Brabham was wrecked at Silverstone and Roger Lea and girlfriend Anita got married in 1969. There followed a short gap in the racing programme while the couple concentrated on building a house on a plot of land and Lea junior really got stuck into the business side of things.

In the mid-seventies, he had a few successes with a Mallock Mk.6B in some clubmans events. This was surprising as he had erroneously used a GT cylinder head (with combustion chambers) in conjunction with concave pistons. It inadvertently reduced the engine's

compression ratio to around 6:1 but he actually managed a fourth place in one race with this ultra-reliable, low-powered set-up...

More racing in Monoposto and Formula Libre events with a March 703 F3 car, fitted with a 1600cc engine, kept him occupied until 1976. That was effectively the end of racing for Roger and Anita (who had been keen enough to spend hours in the pit lane with a stop watch and number board). His father left the family engineering firm in 1973/4 and by 1983 Roger had brought the company where he wanted it to go. It eventually boasted a work force of fifteen when he sold it all off that year.

In an effort to get away from things a bit, the couple bought a sandwich bar in Newquay, Cornwall. This was a raging success for a season, until it was pointed out to them that the concern they'd bought didn't have the relevant food licence... They opened another near Birmingham in 1984 but soon got turned off as the local clientele wasn't in the market for gourmet sandwiches. "Have you got fish 'n' chips? Any pies? What about bangers?" The fry-up trade wasn't exactly what they wanted...

Roger was working with cars again in 1985, when he had the idea of creating a fully type-approved

Mini-based pick-up truck. He went to the extent of building up a complete prototype but received some duff information about full Type Approval costs and procedures for road vehicles. No-one told him that different rules apply to commercial vehicles, so he scrapped the idea as normal passenger vehicle approval would have been too expensive.

This experiment seems to have re-ignited the car designing fever in him and his next idea took root when he saw a load of Bond Bug shells outside the rear of a workshop. "What about a four-wheeled version of that?" he asked himself. In 1989, his Vindicator Concept Coupe arrived at the Newark Alternative and Kit Car Show and it really was a very different kettle of fish. Although Roger could see that the kit car trade was still spreading rapidly in its 'eighties boom, he came to the conclusion that the

Below: A three wheeled Bond Bug gave Roger the idea for his first kit car, the Vindicator Concept Coupe. You can see the influence in this shot around the rear window. Bottom: The Vindicator SR targa-topped smoothie was soon to follow.

Coupe wasn't the right way to go. Interestingly, the 2-litre Pinto powered prototype was then made roadworthy and used daily by Roger's son, Daniel, until a bad accident early in 1990. Badly damaged, the car was then scrapped.

After Newark '89, a flurry of activity erupted in Vindicator Cars' rented premises in Halesowen, West Midlands, as a new car body took shape in very short order. The chassis Roger had designed for the Concept Coupe was essentially retained but the shape became a sleek targa top smoothie resembling the Elan or the Evante in some ways. A prototype mould was made and the first body produced.

This new vehicle was to be called the Vindicator SR (Sports Roadster) and its debut was at the Stoneleigh Kit Cars and Specials Show in 1990. It immediately made a good impression as the first order came in straight away and the next few days saw a couple of deposits taken. This looked like the right recipe for success. Roger went full steam ahead for kit production.

The SR used the Ford Sierra independently suspended rear end, Cortina front suspension components, Ford 2-litre Pinto power and a chassis again derived from the Bond/Concept Coupe project. The full-sized production plug was carefully finalised with Roger's new-found knowledge of GRP moulding processes and the whole thing was shipped off to a mould-maker for an expensive production mould to be properly prepared.

When the moulds and the first shell returned from the GRP sub-contractor, Roger was shocked to find that the job had been terribly done. "The buck was straight and true but the mould was really twisted. It was miles out." This was more than just a snag as the project so far had relieved the Leas of around £30,000 – and much of this had gone into professional mould making.

What to do next? "I went to a solicitor to see if I could get my money from the mould maker. He said that I should basically forget about it because the company in question didn't have sufficient assets to pay me back. I would only get the satisfaction of closing them down and then I'd have to pay my solicitor's fees." That effectively shut down the SR project and all customer deposits, bar one, were refunded.

Retaining its original bodywork, the blue prototype SR was made fully roadworthy in the Vindicator Cars workshop and used by Roger as his personal transport for about six months. The car handled and held the road to high standards and proved great fun to drive. But by the end of 1990 it had been

The very first publicity shot for the Sprint.

deprived of its engine and partially stripped. It was at this time that a local Halesowen man persuaded Roger to part with the body/chassis for the princely sum of £300. Fully rebuilt, Vindicator SR number one was back on the road in 1991.

The one customer deposit retained by Roger was due to the insistence of an extremely keen enthusiast who, regardless of the problems with the GRP bodywork, simply wasn't going to be swayed from his intention to own an SR. The chassis was duly supplied (no problem there) and Roger agreed to release the only bodyshell in his possession. In fact, to improve the shell the front end (its worst deformed area) was cut off and replaced with a new, more uniform moulding made carefully from the 'production' mould by a GRP expert. Thus was completed the only example of the SR to be built other than the prototype.

At least Vindicator SR output had doubled that of the Concept Coupe! Whereas Roger Lea could have been forgiven for being a little depressed about such lack of success, to give the man full credit, he was actually inspired to get stuck in and attempt another project. In fact, while the SR buck had been with the incompetent company making its production moulds, Roger had been at a loose end. He had used this time to make a one-off two-seater sports car for himself and Anita to zoom around in. It also featured Sierra rear suspension components and Cortina front end parts but on a new chassis and with a new Seven-esque body style. It looked OK but his own attempts at moulding were not up

to scratch. Tagged Vindicator Sprint, this two-seater convertible appeared a little prematurely at the Stoneleigh show in 1991 and, despite receiving some criticism due to its poor appearance, met with an unexpectedly enthusiastic response. Through word of mouth, the news got round that the little car existed and a friend of Roger ordered one in August of that year.

After some more attention had been paid to the bodywork side of things, having regrettably ditched the once-promising SR project due to lack of funds, the orders came in a bit more regularly. By the autumn of 1993, Roger had sold nearly 40 examples of the Vindicator Sprint kits. The Vindicator Cars empire had at last made its mark on the kit car scene.

Vindicator Today

Gearing up for production of the Vindicator Sprint kits wasn't all that routine, though. The last 28 sold have the latest chassis version which just happens to be the fourth chassis evolution for the Vindicator. The company boss is pretty industrious when it comes to development and attention to detail. Although his own demonstrator is still the same vehicle that he made in the early days, the production models have

Right and above: The very first production Sprint was a fairly basic affair but showed clear promise for the future with its adventurous suspension set-up. Seats came from an old Triumph TR7.

Above: The Vindicator frame is a substantial affair, quite different from the minimalistic chassis seen on other similar cars. Below left: More recent Sprint already showing development over original car (below).

become much neater.

One owner who has done an outstandingly professional build job on his Sprint is Gordon Freeman. Having cost Gordon in the region of £5000 to make, over a period of five weeks part-time, this example is reportedly the most expensive Vindicator yet. Build budgets are said to be usually in the region of £4000.

If you leave the M5 at Junction 3 and take the A456 towards Kidderminster, the second roundabout you reach after the motorway exit roundabout will probably feature a Vindicator parked at the entrance to The Stables. This is the works which Vindicator Cars rents for production of the Vindicator chassis. Situated at Halesowen, it appears to be an aged farm building but rates about half way up the neatness scale in the kit car trade. The office is ordered and there's room to move about easily!

Vindicator's works takes the form of a long and narrow building, with the rear end set a little higher than the entrance. Alongside the entrance is a small and tidy office adorned with photos of cars linked with the Leas' racing and designing past.

At the very back end of the workshop are the chassis production facilities, welding equipment etc. In the main workshop area, various complete and part-complete cars and kits are to be found. When you take a closer look, it's obvious that these are development models and we'll list some of the new specifications later on in this chapter.

You may have guessed, by the total production figures quoted earlier, that Vindicator is a small scale organisation. No full-time staff are employed but the boss says that there are others who help with the chassis welding when he isn't able to take it all on himself. Anita is often to be found helping out with the office work. Personal and friendly service, therefore, seems guaranteed for the newcomer and for the established customer alike.

Vindicator's supremo has an approachable and enthusiastic personality and is keen to talk Vindicator with all comers. He's very open-minded in his desire to get other people's opinions about his cars and his proposed development work on them. That doesn't detract from his clear grasp of kit packaging priorities.

Value for money and low price are perhaps the most constant themes in his work and the Vindicator Sprint sets out to offer amateur car builders the chance to get something competently finished for less than the cost of the competition.

You either love or hate the Vindicator's styling but Roger is unrepentant about it. In the preamble to the Vindicator price list, he states that "there is a sufficient number of choices available to satisfy the demand for that particular [Lotus Seven] style. Surely one of the reasons for owning a kit car is 'individuality and, good or bad, the Vindicator Sprint *is* different."

Roger and Anita Lea with the latest demonstrator outside the company's small workshop.

139

Whilst not one of the prettiest cars on the market, the Sprint certainly offers the budget enthusiast a good chassis, successful suspension set-up, larger cockpit space and all manner of other value-for-money features.

Current Models

The current Vindicator Sprint is the single model on offer but there is a growing range of options which helps to round off the car's specification, giving plenty more scope to those who have some extra to spend. Things have been made much simpler by Vindicator's choice of independent rear suspension right from the start. This has meant that there isn't a lower budget live axle version. The initial development funds all went towards the one model and this has helped to keep costs down to a sensible level.

What do we find under the skin of the Sprint? Starting from the rear end, there's the full width Sierra IRS. Disc or drum brake Sierra rears are acceptable but modifications are necessary when using the estate donors. "Some customers seem a little worried by the prospect of assembling an independent rear set-up," says Mr. Lea. "Once I explain that it's all a straightforward swap-across from the donor vehicle, things seem a lot clearer and simpler.

"One remarkable aspect of the Sprint is that it does use a large amount of standard parts from the Sierra rear end. Most customers will be using the 1600, 1800 or 2-litre saloon donors in hatchback or Sapphire format. From this, they will take the differential, trailing arms, half-shafts, rear brakes, tubular rear subframe/beam and handbrake assembly complete. Sierra springs and shocks are also a standard fitment.

A special propshaft must be made up by a sub-contractor recommended by the kit manufacturer or by the customer's chosen company. Because of the large engine bay area and the generous bonnet moulding height, the Pinto engine can be easily used, with an after-market air filter, and other four-cylinder engines accommodated quite readily. In fact, the vast majority of customers use the 2-litre Pinto engine and a manual four or five-speed gearbox from the Sierra donor.

An exhaust system for the Pinto is made up using a Cortina/Capri manifold and downpipe, a length of straight tubing and a Mk.3 Escort rear box. Once assembled, this gives you a straight through system underneath the car with an exit at the rear offside.

Vindicator's standard front suspension does not, happily, include the entire Cortina front subframe. Customers wishing to stick to a rigid budget will keep the Cortina upper and lower wishbones, hub/upright assemblies, standard brakes, steering rack, shock absorbers and standard coil springs cut down to around 12.5" free length. This would normally create steering geometry conflicts if the standard subframe was used but Roger has revised the suspension mounts to suit his configuration.

Castor angle at the front has been kept to around 2-4 degrees, using the Cortina standard front tie-rods, but the camber is set 'at 0.5 degrees *positive* to actually reduce overall grip at the front. Zero or negative camber at the front, in the opinion of the designer, would induce too much snap oversteer and would therefore make the Sprint a little tail-happy. Creating a touch of understeer helps to balance things out a bit.

If the customer wants to achieve a high degree of adjustability at the front, there's the option of discarding the Cortina wishbones, springs and shock absorbers in favour of special tubular upper wishbones, adjustable for camber and castor, special tubular lower track control arms (which still accept the Cortina tie rods) and diagonally positioned Spax coil-over shocks. All these parts can be retro-fitted to the same mounting points used by the standard Cortina set-up.

A standard radiator is fitted at a slant, with some coolant pipe lengthening modifications, as it is a fair distance away from the engine. As it happens, the mechanical fan fitted to the car we drove seemed good enough to stave off overheating, even though it was too far from the radiator to have much effect. Air-flow through the radiator and engine bay must be good.

Steering comes courtesy of the standard Cortina rack and column, used in conjunction with an extended lower section. At the driver's end of the column, either Cortina or Sierra column stalks/ignition switch can be used. "The Cortina stalks are a bit long and awkward when you fit a smaller steering wheel. The Sierra alternatives look much neater."

All of these donor parts are mounted to Vindicator's own design of multi-tubular chassis, predominantly using 25mm square section ERW mild steel tube of 1.6mm wall thickness. Some strengthening/stiffening beams in the front suspension mounting area are 3" square with 3mm wall thickness. Of these, the top beam is demountable so that the engine and box can be more easily removed and replaced via the front end of the car.

This cleverly avoids having to lift them out 'upwards' at an extreme angle and to a great height.

Essential beam and torsional rigidity stem from the large backbone section, with additional stiffness from side frames and both bulkheads. The chassis isn't the lightest of the bunch, as its designer has made sure of things by adding a generous quantity of triangulated steel tube. It's physically a big chassis and the car, when seen next to others of its species, is also pretty large.

This has partly been in the interests of housing the tall Pinto SOHC engines and the hefty complete Sierra rear end. Knock-on effects are a large rear boot area with a lockable lid and those curious rear wings which extend a long way to the rear of the wheels. All wings are detachable for quick accident repair etc.

Below: Bonnet is quickly removed for unrivalled access to all the front components. Bottom: Dash design in the current demonstrator certainly looks the part and you can see the use of Sierra column stalk controls.

Soft tops are rarely seen in promotional material, but this shot certainly shows the good practical design of the Vindicator's wet weather gear.

In addition to the steel tubes, which are the self-sufficient structural basis of the chassis, there are extra alloy sheets forming the outer body sides, transmission tunnel, floors, bulkheads, seat backs and dashboard. These can be fitted at the factory for extra cost but they are not designed as structural chassis reinforcements, even if they do have a stiffening effect when in situ.

Currently, the main GRP components are the four wings, the scuttle, the rear boot area with lid and the detachable bonnet/nose moulding. These are supplied in gel coat colours and the later examples appear to be of acceptable quality. Those fitted to the first prototype/demo car certainly weren't much to boast about at all.

Pedals are modified Fiesta parts which are altered to be compatible with the relevant Pinto clutch cable and the Sierra dual-circuit brake master cylinder with servo. Other donor parts to be used are the Mini wiper mechanism complete (but with short arms and blades) and there's the option of using the Mini van fuel tank – if you can get the appropriate fuel take-off union to suit. Otherwise there's the choice of a specially made alloy tank developed for the Sprint.

All of the Cortina parts listed should ideally come from the Mk.4 or 5 models as the Mk.3s have some different components which may not be compatible with the Vindicator. The builder has the choice of using the Sierra or Cortina handbrake lever, with the Sierra handbrake cable assembly, but the overall system incorporates some parts made specially for the Sprint kit.

In the cockpit, there's plenty of room for drivers over six feet tall. There's also a good deal of width at the pedal end of the footwell. This is not, as previously mentioned, a small car. Some builders opt out of the alloy dash standard equipment and fit their own style of wood dash with centre section, complete with neat Triumph Dolomite Smiths gauges.

Subtle black trim and carpet had been expertly fitted and the living area really was quite civilised. There was the optional roll-over bar, which is of a good height for tall occupants but could do with some additional rearwards or forwards bracing due to its height. Contoured seats, with runners, are a luxury which isn't always available in the smaller cars. Elbow, shoulder and leg room are all generous.

Because of the tall roll-over bar, the hood, with its additional single alloy hoop framework, is also of a generous height. Big sidescreens hinge to the sides of the alloy windscreen channel and the leading edge of the hood is affixed to Lift-the-Dot fasteners along the top of the screen frame. Again, neat and fuss-free components of standard quality for the industry.

Out on the road, the 2-litre Pinto-powered Sprint was a completely competent car and very easy to drive. Early impressions were of good stopping power from the servo-assisted brakes, a smooth ride (surprisingly enough) from the Ford springs/shocks and very little body roll. Steering is firm and neutral, with adequate self-centring of the steering wheel. All vital controls are easy to find and use.

Vindicator's dash area is insufficient to cope with line-of-sight main gauges so the speedo and tacho were mounted towards the centre, above the tunnel. This is still common practice for many companies in the field.

With a four-speed gearbox, big boot, quiet exhaust system and smooth springs, this car is an excellent prospect for long-distance touring. It's nowhere near as quick as many of the relatively small and lightweight alternatives available but it fulfils a different role in life. Certainly a good prospect for year-round use, due to its relatively generous proportions.

Performance isn't totally lacking, though. Even if it isn't as quick as a lighter car would be with the same power train, it still has enormous quantities of grip and traction on offer to the energetic driver. All with very predictable handling. A gradual understeer can easily be righted with the throttle and this doesn't instantly invite the rear end to come round and spin away. It'll still show most production cars a clean pair of heels when fitted with a standard 2-litre engine.

Controversy about the Sprint's styling has detracted from the car's very real qualities. It's a subjective area and the public's own perceptions of its looks are the ones that count, not those of the journalist and critic. If the looks detract from potential sales, the price and road manners do the opposite, especially in the grip of a kit-buying recession.

Towards the end of 1993, the Vindicator Sprint kit price was an incredibly reasonable £1295 (no VAT charged as yet), for which customers get the basic kit with separate alloy panels, gel-coloured GRP panels, screen and frame assembled and various other parts and alterations included. That's cheap to say the least. Stage One at £1545 gets you the same but with all the alloy body panels factory fitted and the chassis painted.

With its alloy wheels, decent panel finish and tidy interior, this Vindicator makes a great case for itself in the budget roadster stakes.

This immaculately presented customer's car shows the extent to which even the budget roadster can be taken. Above you can see how the standard Cortina front suspension bolts directly to the Sprint's chassis. Right: 2.1-litre Pinto engine has received lots of attention and is mated to a five speed gearbox driving through a Cosworth Sierra limited slip differential at the back. Serious stuff.

The excellent value Stage Two build offers Stage One specification plus a set of Cortina front suspension components reconditioned and fitted, Sierra rear axle assembly (used) checked and fitted, brake pipes fitted, all GRP fitted and screen fitted for a mere £1975 all-in. (Pretty unbelievable, but true). Add to this the Vindicator 'stage payment' plan and a great deal of personalised flexibility in dealing with customers and you have a good recipe indeed. Don't forget that this is for an independent rear suspension car!

There's a very small list of optional extras. Vindicator Cars doesn't believe in selling customers an incomplete kit and then forcing them to choose from a large selection of 'optionals' which turn out to be essential. "I think that it amounts to cheating," says Roger Lea. Quite right, too.

The Future

There's still a lot happening to improve the range of choice for Vindicator Sprint customers. At the time of our original visit, Roger had already announced the availability of an alternative all-GRP 'wrap-around' (rear and side) body option at extra cost. It features separate front and rear wings for practicality and the alloy original equipment is still offered.

One customer has fitted the very smooth Sierra 2-litre injection Pinto, along with all the requisite tubes, wires and senders. This did necessitate the manufacture of a one-off bonnet bulge to cope with the high plenum chamber.

"If money wasn't a problem," mused Mr. Lea, "I'd carry on developing the original Sports Roadster idea and get it to full kit production." It would be a very attractive vehicle and would undoubtedly be very commercial at the right price.

A return to racing might also be on the cards, again depending upon the available budget. There have been customer enquiries about cars for the Budget and the Super Sports classes of the 750 MC's kit car racing programme. Could we see a high-horsepower Vindicator V8 showing them how it's done on the circuit? Who knows?

Only recently released is the first Sprint build manual. It's not a long and epic tome but there are the salient points to guide the well informed amateur car builder. "It's such a simple car to build that it's pretty obvious where every bit goes." That's fine in some respects – if the builder is at least mechanically literate and can understand the Haynes manual without problems – but Vindicator will still offer copious telephone advice to kit builders. It's all part of the benefit of dealing with a small company.

Official approvals and the other testing processes for seat belt anchorages, welding certification and torsional rigidity remain outside Vindicator's budget until orders start to get really reliable. For the time being, though, the Sprint is in the process of establishing itself as a competent and buildable entry-level kit with a surprisingly high specification.

That Stage Two build is certainly a must for buyers who don't want donor vehicles all over the drive, who don't want to rummage around scrap yards or who haven't got a proper garage for all the necessary assembly work. The Sprint may be unattractive to some but, under the skin, it's a big step forward in low budget kits. The impecunious amateur builder no longer has to put up with the many shortcomings of cars like the once-popular Dutton range, as Vindicator's offerings give you a good deal more in the sophistication stakes. This is positive kit car evolution at work.

Chapter 9

The Others

In the previous eight chapters we've concentrated on the established manufacturers we feel are most actively marketing their various products. These companies will all be operating from proper workshop/factories, they will all have build manuals of one sort or another and they should all have a reasonable stock of the parts you may require throughout the build. They are, in essence, what one might call proper forward-thinking companies you can have confidence in.

But, of course, such is the diversity of the kit industry, that there are all manner of other small companies offering cars that also come under this book's wing as performance roadsters. These might be old companies that have gradually reduced their output over the years, one-man-bands offering highly individual and sometimes quite excellent machines for the lucky few or simply companies that have never aggressively marketed their products within the component car scene. Invariably one finds that the company has hit on a particular type of build construction, odd donor choice or intended use that sets it apart from the more mainstream products dealt with in the previous chapters. What follows is a brief resume of each product.

Just missing out on having its own chapter is the Eldon Autokits roadster. This car originally started life back in late 1990 when an impressive racing car manufacturer, Racecorp Ltd., decided to try its hand at making a road-going lightweight roadster. The Racecorp LA (Light Auto) Roadster was the result and

Eldon Autokits Roadster is a direct descendent of the immensely capable Racecorp LA. A superb spaceframe chassis and well engineered suspension impressed all those who drove the original car.

immediately impressed all those who drove it with its terrific chassis and immaculate presentation. Based on the tried and tested format of a 5-link located Cortina live rear axle and Cortina uprights at the front, the Racecorp was hardly breaking new ground, but it worked well and, combined with the beautifully Tig welded spaceframe chassis and immaculate GRP body, made for a highly impressive package.

The LA was shortly followed by an independent rear suspension model utilising components from the Sierra. The LAi was no less impressive, but perhaps the car's slightly angular styling combined with slow promotion by Racecorp resulted in disappointing sales figures. With the race car side of the company's business taking up an increasing amount of effort, Racecorp put the project up for sale. It was subsequently bought by an existing customer, Phil Surridge, who then spent some time sorting out the project before relaunching it onto the market in late 1993. The ride to date hasn't been an easy one, but Phil's unending enthusiasm for what is a remarkably capable machine should hopefully see his company, Eldon Autokits, into better times.

Top: Cortina based Locust uses a body made from wood mounted on a ladderframe chassis. Simple but strong. Above: Formula 27's spaceframe chassis can be built from plans supplied by the company.

Whilst every kit we've looked at so far in this book (with the exception of Robin Hood Engineering) has been based around a spaceframe chassis with either aluminium or fibreglass bodywork, there are other ways of producing such a machine. The little Locust, marketed by White Rose Vehicles, was originally designed by Moss Cars founder John Cowperthwaite who made a name for himself by designing the JC Midge, a traditional roadster with a wooden body. The advantages to this type of design are numerous but perhaps the most obvious is that the purchaser need only be supplied with some paper plans for the bodywork, which makes for an extremely cheap initial kit purchase. Constructed in the correct way, a wooden body can be extremely strong with further strength and location for the suspension being provided by a simple steel ladderframe chassis. For a smooth exterior finish, the wood can be skinned in a very thin layer of aluminium which can in turn be spray painted.

White Rose Vehicles took on the Locust project from previous owner, T&J Sportscars, and the new company also now owns two of John Cowperthwaite's other designs, the original Midge and more recent Husky jeep. All are constructed out of wood and in the case of the Locust we are talking three-quarter inch plywood which is then skinned in aluminium. White Rose either offers a set of plans or it will supply pre-assembled bodies ready to bolt down onto the chassis. The Locust relies on a simple ladder-frame chassis onto which the immensely strong body is then fixed. More complicated shapes such as the wings and nosecone are supplied in GRP.

The Ford Cortina's double wishbone front suspension is retained in its entirety, while at the back the Locust looks to the ubiquitous Escort to supply its live axle. Engine options also revolve around these two donors but ultimate performance is unlikely to match some of the car's more lightweight competitors.

Because so much of the construction can be left to the purchaser, you'll never find two Locusts the

Above: Citroen 2CV based Falcon Sports may not provide the ultimate in performance but it's certainly cheap. Below: Evergreen Dutton Phaeton has found a new lease of life with Eagle Cars.

same as builders always impose a few of their own personal idiosyncrasies into the design. With the bodywork preassembled by White Rose, the Locust should be a relatively straightforward build and we've seen several really well finished examples.

The BWE Hornet was originally developed by T&J Sportscars to provide a more upmarket version of the Locust. Now under the wing of BWE Sports Cars, the car is in direct competition with its old stablemate. The original idea behind the Hornet was to give the occupant slightly more interior space, so the car is dimensionally bigger than the Locust. Body and chassis construction are almost identical but the Hornet does away with the Cortina's front wishbones and uses its own specially fabricated items. The Cortina live rear axle is also used in preference to the narrower Escort unit.

Taking the plans concept to what must be its natural conclusion, Sterling Autoparts will supply drawings for its Formula 27 from which you can construct your own spaceframe chassis! Thank goodness, those of you not particularly at home with a Mig welder can also order a pre-assembled chassis and the resultant chariot certainly looks none the worse for its humble beginnings. Predominantly aluminium bodywork is accompanied by fibreglass

front and rear wings plus the nose cone. Underpinnings are based around the compact Escort rear live axle which is located by the company's own 5-link suspension. Because of the Escort's strut based front suspension, the Formula 27 resorts back to the Cortina for front uprights and brakes.

The Formula 27, like the previous Hornet and Locust, is very much a kit where the purchaser can choose to do as much or as little of the construction work as he chooses. Depending on your confidence, this is one of the very few kits where you can literally build everything from the chassis upwards.

Another sevenesque vehicle that has found a niche market for itself, this time in the choice of donor, is the Citroen 2CV based Falcon Sports. Utilising the donor's chassis, or a replacement item offered by the kit's manufacturer, Falcon Design, the builder can then choose either a three or four-wheeled version. The Falcon uses all the standard suspension from the 2CV as well as the air-cooled engine. Bodywork is once again a combination of fibreglass wings and ally covered ply (supplied either as plans or as a completed tub). Clearly, performance isn't of paramount importance with the Falcon and the three-wheelers are probably the more commonly ordered version of the kit.

Whilst the Falcon clearly isn't aimed at the balls-out road racer market, the Troll, from Troll Engineering, isn't even aimed at road use! Specialising in the trialing scene, the Troll is another sevenesque vehicle with a very specific aim in life – to get you up the nearest mountain with the least possible fuss. The Troll may be small in size but its specification couldn't be much higher. Basic kits begin at around £6500 while completed cars will set you back nearer £15,000. Not a car for the budget enthusiast. As you might expect, the Troll returns to the more conventional construction of a spaceframe chassis with aluminium and fibreglass bodywork.

Whilst the car has been designed with trials in mind, lower suspension settings are available to those wanting to hit the back roads and here the car's 1600cc X-flow engine (the only option available) will give it plenty of urge. A highly specialised but beautifully crafted machine for the fortunate few.

As we begin to hit the outer limits of what could realistically be contained within this book's pages, there is just perhaps room for such creatures as the Eagle P21. Better known as the Dutton Phaeton, this relic from the late seventies and early eighties was the archetypal budget performance roadster of the day and it has received a new lease of life under the wing of Eagle Cars. Whilst retaining the Ford donor, Eagle

Mid-engined CC Cyclone takes the Lotus Seven theme on to new boundaries. Who knows whether it will achieve the same success?

has updated the chassis and body to produce a car of better quality than the sometimes slightly shabbily produced originals.

Since the Lotus Seven was originally launched, there have always been those trying to retain the excitement of the minimalist roadster yet update the design. Few have succeeded (which explains the wide selection of cars which follow a similar design concept) but there are still one or two kits currently on offer that can justifiably lay claim to updating the Lotus Seven design.

Perhaps the most exciting is the recently launched Cyclone, from Car Craft of Lytham St. Annes, Lancs. Utilising a mid-mounted 2-litre Vauxhall engine, the little Cyclone is causing quite a sensation with its combination of vivid acceleration, superb handling and immaculate road manners. A spaceframe chassis locates Vauxhall front uprights (from the earlier front engine/rear drive models) and brakes on specially fabricated wishbones while at the rear the front engine/front-wheel-drive driveshafts are retained along with modified hub carriers located on Car Craft's own trailing arm set-up. Lotus was one of the first companies to appreciate the mid-engined layout and its use here has succeeded in giving the Cyclone pin-sharp steering response, terrific grip and superb balance.

Others also exploring the mid-engined roadster theme include the wacky Midtec Spyder; the as yet untried but extremely promising Montego-engined Imola; the viciously quick Brooke ME190; the superbly detailed and highly individual BMW motorbike engined Grinnall Scorpion and the recently launched Dax Kamala. All offer lightweight minimalist thrills and all, to a greater and lesser extent, do indeed offer what might be considered a modern interpretation of the Lotus Seven concept. Only time will tell whether they have captured the hearts of enthusiasts to the same degree as the mighty Lotus.

WHERE TO GET FURTHER INFORMATION

CATERHAM SEVEN
Caterham Cars, Seven House, Town End, Caterham Hill, Surrey.
Tel: 01883 346666.

TIGER SUPER SIX
Tiger Cars Ltd., 2A Penhall Road, Charlton, SE7 8RX. Tel: 0181-293 1103.

SYLVA STRIKER
Sylva Autokits Ltd, Unit A11, Dowlands Business Park, Manby, Louth, Lincoln LN11 8UT.
Tel: 01507 328809.

WESTFIELD
Westfield Sportscars Ltd., 1 Gibbons Industrial Park, Dudley Road, Kingswinford, West Midlands DY6 8XF. Tel: 01384 400077.

ROBIN HOOD
Robin Hood Engineering Ltd., Oxclose Lane, Mansfield Woodhouse, Notts NG19 8DF.
Tel: 01623 422286.

DAX RUSH
DJ Sportscars International, 2 Edinburgh Place, Edinburgh Way, Harlow, Essex CM20 2DJ.
Tel: 01279 442661.

VINDICATOR SPRINT
Vindicator Cars, The Stables, Hayley Green Farm, Hagley Road, Halesowen, West Midlands B63 1DZ.
Tel: 0121 585 5627.

ELDON
Eldon Autokits, Unit 32, Eldon Way, Paddock Wood, Tonbridge, Kent TN12 6BE.
Tel: 01892 838683.

LOCUST
White Rose Vehicles, Upbury Manor Centre, Marlborough Road, Gillingham, Kent ME7 5HT.
Tel: 01634 281736.

BWE HORNET
BWE Sports Cars, 13 Knowsley Street, Barnsley, South Yorkshire S70 6ET.
Tel: 01226 293717.

FORMULA 27
Sterling Autoparts, Newlands Farm, Bourne Lane, Brimscombe, Stroud, Gloucestershire GL5 2RQ.
Tel: 01453 886223.

FALCON SPORTS
Falcon Design, 8 Whitworth Road, Frome, Somerset BA11 4BY.
Tel: 01373 473695.

TROLL
Troll Engineering, 15 The Parade, Minehead, Somerset TA24 5NL.
Tel: 01643 703721.

EAGLE P21
Eagle Cars Ltd., Hooe Farm Industrial Estate, Tye Lane, Walberton, Arundel, Sussex BN18 0LU.
Tel: 01245 544673.